"*Lessons and Carols* fearlessly examines ideas about innocence, resentment, loss, and renewal, asking, can we actually change or are we doomed to repeat the same mistakes forever? John West's pursuit of truth and beauty in this book is both masterful and unforgettable."

—CHELSEA HODSON
author of *Tonight I'm Someone Else*

"'This happened,' John West writes at the end of one chapter. 'It is also a metaphor.' His words might serve as an epigraph for his frank, edgy, hopeful story about recovery and slippage and squalor and eruptions of love and sudden epiphanies. These nine memorable 'lessons and carols' take us through episodes in an unsettled life interrupted by faith, love and a baby. For those who have struggled with addiction or depression, and those who love them, this is a gritty, gutsy, unabashed and surprising book about hope."

—MARILYN MCENTYRE
author of *Caring for Words in a Culture of Lies*
and *When Poets Pray*

LESSONS
AND
CAROLS

A Meditation
on Recovery

John West

WILLIAM B. EERDMANS PUBLISHING COMPANY
GRAND RAPIDS, MICHIGAN

Wm. B. Eerdmans Publishing Co.
4035 Park East Court SE, Grand Rapids, Michigan 49546
www.eerdmans.com

Book design by Lydia Hall

Printed in the United States of America

29 28 27 26 25 24 23   1 2 3 4 5 6 7

ISBN 978-0-8028-8249-3

Library of Congress Cataloging-in-Publication Data

A catalog record for this book is available from the Library
of Congress.

For Galen and Lavinia

And for those who struggled

And for those who are struggling still

JOHN ASHBERY

As philosophers have often pointed out, at least / This thing, the mute, undivided present, / Has the justification of logic, which / In this instance isn't a bad thing.

CONTENTS

PROLOGUE

The past unfolds into the present like a flower opening its petals, revealing its gold-dusted center. Like, *in the beginning was the Word*, and then, suddenly, a baby is born in a stable, and then the beginning's meaning arrives, pollen borne on a bee's body. At night, when the flowers in my yard cover their faces while the moon gilds them silver, nothing exactly changes, except the past promises *tomorrow* instead of *today*.

I walk out of the psychiatric ward two weeks before Christmas. In the parking lot, the waning moon looks for a place to hide from the midmorning sun, brightening piles of half-melted snow. In the car, on the way home, I make myself a deal. No, I never have to put myself back there—in writing or in life. Yes, I have to get better.

In the beginning, the Lessons and Carols is a wooden shack and a story. It is December of 1880, and Bishop Edward White Benson, who would later become the archbishop of Canterbury, hatches a scheme to keep his congregants engaged over Christmas while the grand Gothic Revival cathedral at Truro is under construction. His son: *My father arranged from ancient sources a little service for Christmas Eve—nine carols and nine tiny lessons.* The lessons are snippets of Bible verses, stretching from original sin to Christ's birth. In 1919, King's College in Cambridge adapts and produces the Lessons and Carols with new works for organ and choir. It becomes an institution, happens every year, leaps from church to church, travels across radio waves and continents.

When I arrive at my off-campus apartment, I pack clothes and books and toiletries so I can go back to my parents' home for the Lessons and Carols at my childhood church. A year before, almost to the day, I gathered some friends in my tiny apartment, and we enacted the Lessons and Carols like we weren't atheists. I make myself another deal. No, I won't re-create the Lessons and Carols this year. Yes, I will every year after.

THE FIRST LESSON

Here is your garden; keep it well.

Genesis 2:15

Caring for this baby has taught me new ways to resent. Other people tell me things—absurd things, things about seeing with baby's eyes, etc.—and I resent that I do, in fact, sometimes see with baby's eyes.

Like in the morning, when a blue-gray bird whose name I don't know preens on my white picket fence. When there are titters I've never noticed before from the swallows in the oak. When, once, Galen and I spy a mourning dove in the cemetery near our house. I mean, honestly.

I often say that summer is the most desirable season, but, I confess, I wish it were winter. I wish the moon weren't an abstract expressionist hurling silver onto my neighbor's oak, watching its handiwork drip down onto my short-cut grass. I wish the baby were older. I wish I were older, were not resentful (*re* and *sent*: feeling again) all the time. But I am resentful, and she is still a baby, and the moon—yes, hello moon!—is just as annoyingly beautiful as ever.

I want to buy a book about birding, so that I can identify that regal blue-gray one. I think I would notice him more—or at least notice more about him—if he had a name. Of course, he already has a name; I just don't know it. This is exactly my problem when we find out about the baby, when the case worker calls to tell us that she is five days old.

"We don't have a car seat," I say.

"Target's open." I can hear the smile in her voice.

That afternoon, as we leave Target with a cartful of baby things, we get sent a picture. A tuft of thin black hair, dark skin, a green, semitransparent pacifier like a small moon almost eclipsing her improbably round face. We call the hospital from the Target parking lot to ask if she's getting attention. The nurse laughs.

"The doctors fight over who gets to feed her," she says. "She's a perfect baby."

Here are some of the things that require names in Genesis: *Air fowl. Field beasts. The gathering of waters. Dry land. A ground-tiller. A sheep-keeper. The cattle-havers. The tent-dwellers. The iron-and-brass artificers. The harp-and-organ handlers. Light. Darkness. The firmament. An eastward-goer. All living creatures. Her.*

Before we meet her, we call the hospital every day. We cannot go because of the pandemic.

"She's such a love," a nurse says.

"She's a great baby," a doctor says.

"She's so strong," an occupational therapist says.

Though I haven't met her yet, I agree with all of them. She must be strong as an ox, as solid as a ground-tiller. I want nothing more than to surround her with stories of her own resilience. I hope we get the chance.

Writing in the present tense is a way to avoid resentment, a paradox through which I crawl inside my resentment, so far down, I cease to feel *again*, but rather inhabit the moment I felt the first time, the spring that feeds resentment, which isn't resentment at all but just what it was like *to be*.

Of course, the lie of the present tense is that the me that felt *first* and the me that felt *again* are the same. In life, they are not the same, but on the page, without the past, these selves collapse into a point from which narrative distance cannot escape. But even though critics don't like present tense, just like they don't like the verb *to be*, I chose it for a reason.

For example, parenting is like the present tense in that it transforms resentment into something with words and a spine. Mornings with her, awake before the sky is light, are a species of blessing—an Old Testament blessing of the kind you might not want. A blessing that cracks ground, water pushing up and out.

Things I resent include my depression (always so boring). My stolid, plodding lack of hypomania (once so exciting). The fact that I miss my hypomania (am I a monster?). Thoughts of my own monstrousness (can I be redeemed?). The concept of the present tense.

Resentment's floodwaters have swept away so much of what I've tried to build. But maybe then, suddenly, everything changes.

I am fluttering on the edge of a couch in the dorm's common room, the youngest here, a mascot. I am on my second glass of wine. A body passes before the spindly light, and the shadows lurch into a different form. A glass or two later, I am not so nervous.

A man in his twenties sits across the room from me on a stained love seat. The soprano is draped on his arm, and she is bending forward, laughing without dignity. He smirks at his own wit. His eyes catch mine, and the smile that takes his face would devour me. I want to be eaten.

I am ignoring the talk around me to hold eye contact with this man when the wine in my throat and stomach solidifies. I stand up too quickly, walk to the door.

Then, suddenly, the man is beside me.

"Going home?" he asks.

My whole body is tingling. "Walk me?" I reply.

In the long field between the rows of dorms, he puts his hand on my forearm.

"Look," he says, and I look at the dark, mountain-shaped hole in the night jutting out over the end of the field. I look at the moonlight draped on the branches of a tree, at the shadow splashed across the tall grass. He leans toward me, like kisses are just things that anyone might give to anyone else at any time. I have never been kissed. Neon fireflies flare in the dark like the tips of cigarettes.

The next few evenings, I cycle through different dorms, different common rooms. A gulp of gin and tonic here, a half inch of scotch there. Each night, I crisscross the field to find the man who kissed me. Each evening that I find him, blushes bloom across my face. We don't kiss again.

I learn about hangovers from the birds that scream outside my window.

I am pretending to be a gay teacher at a boarding school who is in an illicit relationship with one of his students, but I am really a confused eighteen-year-old in a relationship—my first—with one of my female castmates. When I vigorously kiss the man who plays my student, the crowd goes wild, hooting and catcalling. He is handsome, older, experienced, and gay in the way that I envy: without apparent shame. But I am not aroused when I kiss him.

At one of the semiregular cast parties that come to dominate my social life, my girlfriend and I hunt for a place to do shots. The rest of the cast is scattered through the living room, where the sparse furniture is all fire-retardant and looks it. The institutional carpet is rough on my bare feet, and the sounds of other parties seep in through the just-open windows. We giggle as we weave our way through the mess of castmates and castmates' friends back to the kitchen. She heaves open the freezer, her face flushed, and we extract orange juice concentrate and a thin plastic bottle of vodka. We take turns pouring vodka into a shot glass and finishing it with a spoonful of concentrate. It tastes awful. Sam's hair is buzzed short. She kisses my cheek.

She smokes pot, and I hate pot, but I smoke it anyway. One night, just after we are done passing the adeptly rolled joint between us, we lie on the weathered slats of wood in her attic. I watch the streetlight cut a shadow across her face while she strips off her shirt. Then my fingers are in her mouth, and time has dilated. I kiss the mark in the exact center of her breasts.

Her off-campus house perpetually out of glasses, we drink vodka from bowls.

Then, suddenly, Sam tells me she's not going to buy me any more alcohol.

"I don't understand," I say.

Then, suddenly, we are walking around the pond in the center of the arboretum just off campus where snow muffles the crunch of leaves and twigs. She is breaking up with me. I make another circuit of the pond after she leaves.

At the on-campus bar, I drink from others' pitchers of beer. I kiss a woman whose locs smell like vanilla. When I stumble back to my dorm room, I look at the torn receipt, her phone number scrawled on it. I throw it out and fall asleep to my roommate's breathing.

I meet a black-haired conductor of music at a party, a senior. He is drinking red wine from a glass with a delicate stem. I am drinking gin from a coffee mug, clutching at it with both hands. When he asks if I'd like a cigarette, his too-steady eyes don't leave mine. His light songlike words don't match the hard set of his face.

Then we are outside, and his hand is at my throat, and his tongue is in my mouth. I break off the kiss to breathe, and he pushes me against the stucco wall of the house. I feel the small points of plaster scratch my back, the birdlike flutter in my chest. The streetlight shines yellow off his hair, his glasses, and his tongue is in my mouth once more, but I reach my hand out. I push him away.

Later, when I am alone in my dorm room, I close my eyes, and he pushes me against the stucco wall over and over. The bird in my chest flutters each time.

I never want to see him again.

I have a running joke with Gabe that we should cut down a Christmas tree from the fields north of campus. What makes it a joke is that I am a dedicated rule follower; I rarely even speed. But the night before my Lessons and Carols, I park my car at the edge of the northernmost parking lot on campus. I try not to look suspicious as I trudge away from the road. The clouds shift, and the moon brightens the snow all at once. This is a terrible idea. I lie down at the base of a small, Charlie Brown–esque tree, and I take a saw out of my bag with shaking hands. Snow creeps in at my ankles and wrists. My neck grows sore. On the way back, I worry about tracks, so I don't drag the tree, which is surprisingly heavy.

When I imagined this transgression, I didn't think about the weight of the tree. The flat, empty white of the field, too big. The pine resin, sticky on my fingers. The smell of it in my nose, coating my throat. My breath feral in my ears.

Later, I smile and tell Gabe about the tree, say it fell off the back of a truck and ended up in my apartment—a Christmas miracle. He laughs and asks if I'm crazy.

The day of the party, I go to the library and print out the play, which I have toiled over, revising and abbreviating— why does Eve come from Adam's rib, and what are Abraham and Sarah doing in the Christmas story at all? I make fifteen copies, and the woman behind me in line stares at the cover sheet, incredulous.

The flower shop sells mistletoe. I have never actually seen the stuff. I hang it just inside the door of my little apartment. When my friends arrive, all dressed up, I am the consummate host—putting jackets on my bed, bustling back to the kitchen for more dinner preparations. When Ellen arrives, I point to the sprig of mistletoe, and we kiss. I worry about the ham in my tiny oven—almost like a child's oven. We prop the front door open to keep the sweat at bay. Sonia arranged a Secret Santa. I play the keyboard, and we sing carols—Gabe bellows triumphant during "Good King Wenceslas." I am the narrator. David plays God. Alice is Mary. We are all atheists.

We read from John: *And the light shone in the darkness, and the darkness did not overcome it.*

In the dark room, we hold up our lit candles in silence. They flutter in the draft of the open window, and I close my eyes at the reprieve.

The next year, Gabe will find me drunk in my apartment. I will return to a psychiatric ward.

CAROL

For E

Hunching in a corner of the narrow courtyard of this rehab facility, B bums me cigarettes because I ran out. Rain falls around us, wilting his curly hair, and we talk about what we used to be like, how we just don't know what we'll do when we get out of here.

E has a crush on B. B seems at least as taken with E as I am with the pair of them. I've never been somewhere before where I've wanted to let the platonic and erotic overlap, and finally, I see the appeal, but I don't trust this world where love can take you at any moment.

E teaches me to play spades. I almost never take a trick.

We aren't allowed any personal music players, but there is a radio on the unit. During the evening free time, when we are allowed to turn it on, I listen to whatever station the others want. But once a week, a few of us are driven to an LGBT-friendly meeting of Alcoholics Anonymous a few blocks from my parents' home, and then we listen to whatever radio station we want.

Before one meeting, I use my phone time to request a Sufjan Stevens song from the DJ of the best local radio station. I tell him everything: we're in rehab, and if he could play this song that we all love during the half hour that we're in transit to the meeting, we'd love him forever. He laughs. He says he'll see what he can do. Later, driving through the neighborhood I grew up in, the song comes on. So, feeling the joy of it, after the meeting, as we stand around and drink the burned coffee, B, E, and I try to flirt with the other men, and, haltingly, with each other.

We go to the local YMCA, and B and I make a slow circuit of the track while everyone else plays basketball. Both of us are out of shape and smokers, so our words come out in quick bursts followed by long pauses. Sweat mats our hair. We blush in the back of the van on the way back to rehab, our hands touching, back to back, on the seat between us.

Later, with ugly carpeting at our feet and ugly light in our eyes and ugly art on the wall, E puts his arm through my arm and we skip up and down the hallway until a harried counselor tells us to stop.

And I know that wanting love does not mean wanting sex does not mean wanting a drink does not mean wanting greatness, but they are bound up for me, a game I invented, whose rules led me here. So, I will not kiss B. I will not kiss E. I want to. The want never sated, maybe insatiable, maybe I am Tantalus in a hell of my own devising.

Later, I play a concert in a tiny room. After the concert, B warns me, but it's too late. I see E's eyes, his pupils wrong, his body language wrong, everything wrong.

"Are you high?" I ask.

"No," he lies.

My eyes are drawn to his pinprick pupils, little black holes.

I glance at B, who throws his arm around E and leads him outside, into the bright afternoon. I won't see him again.

The Latin poet Catullus was born in 84 BCE. One of his poems, the one scholars number 101, he wrote as an elegy for his brother. I do not read Latin. But when people die or disappear, I try to write them a fresh translation of Catullus's elegy. In this book, I have made these my carols.

But translation is a lossy process. Take a screenshot of a picture. Take a screenshot of that. Take a screenshot of that. Watch it degrade in each iteration. *Loss*. I tell N that I know he brought the booze to that girl's party where we all got kicked out, and he says he'll take a piss test if that's what it takes, and then he's dead. *Loss*. A and I wake early, sip coffee from travel mugs on our way to take a modern dance class together, and then one day she doesn't call back, and then her internet profiles wink out, one by one, and then her number stops working. *Loss*.

Robert Hass: *All the new thinking is about loss. / In this it resembles all the old thinking.* I read somewhere that young people always think they invented sex. I sometimes feel I invented mourning. This is foolish. I've read Catullus. I know I didn't invent mourning, but, having broken a person down to their component memories, I can't help but feel that I've discovered something when the parts do not make a whole.

AFTER CATULLUS

This world is not mine. I travel it anyway. / Suddenly, I'm at your tomb, / Where I, myself, lay death-gifts. / I, alone, ask questions. / Of course, you do not answer. / How senseless the violence of fate, which has cleaved us. / And all I have is ritual—and tears.

THE SECOND LESSON

"Here is a promise," the angel said.

Genesis 22:15–18

I don't resent the baby. Not really. Sometimes, in the morning, I take her outside and lay her on a padded blanket on the ground. She makes little vocalizations as though she wants to talk to me, and tenderness runs across my face like a bramble of plump blackberries.

In college, I used to wake up early, early enough to be the first person in line when the little cart that sold ham and cheese pastries opened, early enough to be known to its employees, early enough that I could sit with a crossword on the bench outside and smoke.

Things have changed since then. I try to make the pastries, which never turn out. I print off a Wednesday puzzle, which is now beyond me. But I still fondly remember the round, full sensation of the cigarette smoke in my throat, so maybe things haven't changed that much. Or, maybe one day you smoke a pack a day; then, suddenly, you don't.

But that story is as much a lie as any other arc that bends toward anything—like you can elide the middle, like there is a beginning, a middle, and an end—as much true as not true.

Because *then* and *suddenly* are lying words. Nothing changes. Things become more like what they already were. But what, exactly, were they already?

When I was younger, I sat in my first ever sponsor's bright, tidy apartment and listened to him instruct me on how to turn my resentments upside down, pull them inside out, see what might be in there. His music stand held Telemann. On his bedside table, a bottle of lube sat unabashed. This is exactly what I wanted: to be unashamedly, unapologetically myself. But we were always talking about resentment, and I know now what it is that he wanted to show me. Resentment is also a name for a memory left too long in a warm, damp place.

I won't always be resentful because some part of my soul—
what a Christian word!—already is not, in fact, resentful.
This I have to believe. One day, mouthing curses, Saul went
journeying, *and suddenly there shined round about him a
light from heaven, and he fell to the earth. And when Saul
arose from the earth, when his eyes were opened, he saw no
man. They led him by the hand, and brought him into Da-
mascus. He was there three days without sight, and neither
did he eat nor drink.* The truth of the conversion is that the
other Saul was already there, painted over, ready for God's
light to strip him clean, blind him, ready to need neither
food nor water.

So, one of my least favorite questions is *what happens
in your book?*

"You know, say it like *this happens, then this happens,*"
a friend encourages.

"I know," I say. "I'll try." But I don't want to try.

I suppose that what happens is that I resent a lot. I suppose that what happens is that, *then* and *suddenly,* I don't.

A vexing question for philosophers: Does language reflect the world out there or does it distort the world—create it, even?

Ludwig Wittgenstein wrote his *Tractatus Logico-Philosophicus* and, believing he solved philosophy, retired to the mountains for almost a decade—even taught in a village school—before coming back to solve philosophy again. He wrote, often, in little fragments. In *On Certainty*, he grappled with the question of how he knows (or if he knows) that he has hands. *The propositions which one comes back to again and again as if bewitched—these I should like to expunge from philosophical language.*

What lives in the heart of a name? What lives in the heart of a word? If you change a connotation, a referent, when does one thing become something different altogether? These questions I should like to expunge from my language. But who would I be without them?

I wouldn't mind expunging that question either.

I never imagined that I would see in a child—i.e., a person who is not me—my resentments reflected back to me. I never imagined I would see those questions I should like to expunge given physical form, a form with which I fall in love. This baby will grow into what she already was, though her future remains unknowable. We aren't what we were till we become what we will be.

I am eighteen years old, turning pages for the organist-choirmaster of this grand Congregationalist church, and I am falling asleep on a stool behind the screen that separates the organ console from the rest of the sanctuary. The minister is delivering a sermon I would probably appreciate if I weren't so tired. The organist nudges me, and my eyes flick open, up to the stained glass window of a virgin Mary and a baby Jesus. On Christmas Eve, they turn on a light so that Mary and Child are illuminated as though by some warm inner fire. Dark wood frames the window, and white plaster frames the wood. Then the rows of organ pipes ripple outward. Triumphant music will erupt from them shortly, and I will turn the pages dutifully, and I will go home and drink the contents of my parents' liquor cabinet, and I will smoke a cigarette or two on the roof of their house.

I fill a heavy glass with something amber, slide open the window from my attic room to the tarry shingles, and slither out. Looking down at the quiet streets of Minneapolis, I light a cigarette, inhale, and feel my muscles relax. The minister calls the sacraments *an outward sign of an inward grace*. I wonder what else besides grace leaves marks.

The organist, musically incredible and somewhat eccentric, demands perfection. During rehearsals, when his choir—amateur ranks swelled by professional soloists—misses a passage in a Bach chorale, he cuts them off with an arm wave, claps his hands together.

"Again," he says—all business. When the altos fall off their line, he hums loudly till they slide back up.

Talking with one of my parents' friends after services, somewhere near the exact middle of the sanctuary, I ask why there isn't a cross with Jesus on it, like in churches in the movies. I've been going to church my entire life and never thought to ask this.

"That's a Catholic thing," my parents' friend says. He points up toward the screen and choir. Turning slowly, he points left, toward a neat little row of pews. He keeps turning, and I follow with my eyes. He points back toward the main entrance of the sanctuary, three sets of doors, where a gaggle of congregants gossips. Finally, he points right, toward the inversion of the left. "The entire sanctuary is in the shape of a cross," he says.

Form is content. The medium is the message. I'm standing over Jesus's still heart, and what's the point of art, if not this?

Jason, a Catholic friend of mine, asks where I go to church. We're walking around a Minneapolis lake on a day when the sky is the kind of blue that can't be reproduced. Jason's pants are too short, and his posture is too straight, but I find he cuts a strangely majestic figure. He has an encyclopedic knowledge of the kinds of highbrow cultural trivia that others find impressively, if uselessly, smart. Like, he's read Ovid. A year or two ago, he wrote a poem that contained a line about *libidinous fireflies*. He's a better musician than I am. He gets better grades too. He's a Republican, though, so I guess you can't have it all. When I tell him about our Congregational church, he nods, satisfied, as though this fact speaks to some secret truth about my soul. He's always been a little smug about religion, though I know he means well. He goes to a church whose mass is still in Latin, Vatican II be damned.

"You're a Calvinist, then," he says.

"Am I?" I look out across the lake, oddly shaped. It's narrow where we're walking, and I can see the dots of people strolling along the other side.

"You should know." He laughs. Despite myself, I've harbored a crush on him since middle school.

"I don't think we believe in predestination or anything like that. At least I don't," I lie. We have just learned about the Reformation in our high school's world history class. I can't remember the other theological fault line— something about what the communion bread and wine really turn into. These kinds of arguments seem impossibly far away, trivial, seen through the back end of a set of binoculars. I can't get worked up about them. No, what I want to get worked up about are the big things. I want to get worked up about God. About greatness and art.

I decide to get worked up about painting, but skill eludes me despite near-constant practice. I rush through lunch or use my free period or stay late after school to slip into the art classroom. The art teacher doesn't seem to mind.

I spend a couple of nights without sleep, but I don't want to sleep, and I paint all the time, even at home. When I fall asleep—finally—it is during my free period, in a warm corner of the room my high school uses as an art gallery. A teacher wakes me up and takes me to see the counselor. She asks how I'm feeling, and I don't understand the question.

That night, after dark, I sit on a bench in the park where I used to sled as a child and try to make sense of the counselor's question. I would say I feel *sad*, but if I open the door to the room that holds the feeling, I am convinced it will spill out and crush me. I sip from a beer and decide it's better not to think much more about it.

Then, suddenly, I am scoring my arms with a razor blade because I don't know what else to do, but I know that this signals pain.

One night, I drive to Saint Paul, to the High Bridge that spans the dark river and the dark pines and the dark buildings on the riverfront, and I call my best friend from the car. He's on a date. I don't know what I say, but he and his date come, and we walk across the bridge together, as if to say, *See, you can cross without jumping.*

I've cried before from this feeling. But when he hugs me at the midpoint of the bridge, looking down at the Mississippi, my tears feel like they're building something, pooling yellow in the streetlights, a placid spring that might sustain me. His girlfriend drives his car, and he drives mine, and he takes my hand in his before I go inside to tell my parents that I don't know how to kill myself, but I know I want to die.

My parents and I talk, and I am checked into an adolescent psychiatric ward.

Years later, I walk all across Chicago, down to the lakefront park, to see the Bean. Technically, the sculpture is named *Cloud Gate*, but enormous and mirrored, it looks like a giant silver reflective bean. There I am in the Bean's mirror, but it is not me. I am scrunched up, distorted, my middle collapsing into a single point. I move to the left, and the same point balloons outward until my love handles grow misshapen. Each step I take transforms the image that reflects back to me. I pose before it, a coffee in my gloved hand, smiling while the wind thrashes around me and reddens my nose and cheeks. Galen snaps a picture.

The Renaissance painter Parmigianino looked into a convex mirror and drew himself, distorted. Then the twentieth-century poet John Ashbery wrote his own self-portrait by looking at Parmigianino's painting. At the Bean, I want to see as Parmigianino saw, but I'm no painter. I want to memorize Ashbery's poem, but it's too long. What I really want is to arrange a room full of others' work—a whole salon wall of convex mirrors—and glimpse myself in every one.

Galen and I go to hear a reading by the poet and classicist Anne Carson. Waiting in the library's pink marble hallway, the man in line before us explains to the woman in line before him that the word *essay* comes from the French *to try*. Galen rolls her eyes. We move forward slowly, and then the hallway opens onto a circular foyer. A tiny, mirrored Bean rests in a glass case, a perfect replica of *Cloud Gate*. I pose before this replica, holding a coffee in one hand. I point with the other. Galen snaps another picture. John Ashbery: *The words are only speculation / (From the Latin* speculum, *mirror): / They seek and cannot find the meaning of the music.* Carson's writing is an attempt, a seeking. I would like to seek, though I wouldn't mind finding the meaning in the music. I, too, would like to write essays in a convex mirror.

In September of 1708, the mayor of Mühlhausen, Germany, is about to die. While he lies on his deathbed reading *ars moriendi*, Lutheran literature on the art of dying, a bright young composer named Johann Sebastian Bach is writing the mayor's funeral cantata, *Actus tragicus*.

When he dies, the town turns out. Sitting in the church, light streaming in through the stained glass, they hear two seemingly incompatible versions of life, one truth and then another: *We all must die* and *We all live forever in Christ*.

The voices enter. *God's time is the best of all times*, they sing. The instruments punctuate their weaving, quick-moving lines, triumphant. *In him, we live, move, and are, as long as he wills*. Then, suddenly, the voices slow—time itself slows—their lines become mournful: *In him, we die at the appointed time, when he wills*.

Bach is trying to reconcile a paradox. *Today you will be with me in paradise*, the tenor sings. Then the alto joins, etching a popular hymn above the tenor, a kind of Baroque-era sample. *As God has promised me: death has become my sleep*. The two tunes, the two images of life, are fused in his creation.

I play the first recorder for *Actus tragicus* at an Early Music festival. Dressed in our least rumpled performance clothes, my friends and I shuffle into a beautiful church with a small circle of abstract stained glass above the altar and rosy wood floors and pews. We begin to play.

It happens in the exact middle of the piece: a perfect aria, a synthesis of life and death, the two presented one on top of the other like two transparencies on a projector. The tenor begins a fugue. Then the alto takes it, transposed up. The bass follows, transposed down. *All flesh waxeth old as a garment: for the covenant from the beginning is, Thou shalt die the death*. Our soprano enters. *Ja, komm, Herr Jesu!* she implores. (*Yes, come, Lord Jesus!*) She sings alone, begging for his presence, and then the fugue begins again. This time, as they sing about the covenant we've made, about our inevitable deaths, the soprano's voice floats above, calling Jesus down. When the sound dies away, in the rich emptiness, I glimpse something out there. Grace and terror. Anne Carson: *Nothing vast enters the lives of mortals without ruin.*

On a video call, I play the piano for LC, singing (badly) the tune of a piece I am writing using their words. They listen patiently, and at the end, they ask about a passage, why *this* chord and not *that* chord. I am befuddled. I tell them about what I see in their poem, about the double-yolked self, and they laugh.

"John," they say. "I don't want you to explicate my poem; I want you to explicate your song."

The song is your poem; I just gave it a new context, I want to say. How much does a context need to change before one poem is a different poem altogether?

I tell a friend that I'm a bad Christian. "Half the time I don't even want to believe, and the other half, I don't really believe, I just want to," I say. "I really was just in it for the music."

She laughs from her belly. "You gotta find something out there."

So, later, as I go about my business, I listen to Bach's cantatas. I want to hear them like I used to. In a church where the sun, slowed by the colors of the stained glass, inches its way across the pews. Like an outward sign of some inward grace. Like an essaying, an attempt, a seeking. Like the soprano's voice arcing across the sanctuary, imploring, *Komm, Herr Jesu, komm.*

Then I am in a diner off Sixth Avenue in Manhattan, holding an oversize, multipage menu, trying to remember why I let Galen talk me into extending our Thanksgiving in this godforsaken city for an extra week. The light from the window is joyous. Blue sky. Perfect, coloring-book clouds. LC is across the table. I woke up five minutes before my alarm, and I've already drunk three cups of coffee sitting on a bench in Washington Square Park, where an optimistic busker played a saxophone rendition of "What a Wonderful World" in the crisp early-morning air. New York is showing off for me. I still don't like being back here.

Now LC is explaining a theory: your favorite Christmas tune describes your soul. They've told me this theory before, I'm fairly sure, but I can't remember what I said.

"What's your favorite?" they ask.

"There are too many good ones," I protest, stalling for time. "I couldn't possibly pick just one."

LC will not be deterred.

"How about 'Have Yourself a Merry Little Christmas'—the one where Judy Garland is basically crying?" I was just saying it, but it's the truth—or at least *a* truth. I've watched that part from *Meet Me in St. Louis* about a thousand times, though I've never seen the movie in its entirety. Watching the clip, I see Garland's eyes shine with tears. Mine shine too, every time.

"That's my favorite too!" Their enthusiasm is contagious, even this early, even in this concrete trap of a city. "Sad Christmas is the best Christmas," they confide.

"It's real Christmas," I say.

The thing that's *sad* about Christmas is its premise: we're fallen and need redemption. The thing that's *real* about Christmas is that this premise is probably true: I thirst to be redeemed. But I'm not sure that this makes *real, sad* Christmas the *best* Christmas.

CAROL

For C

I sit with C at the halfway house on the metal chairs at the metal table in the courtyard with rocks that are strewn about haphazardly, as though by a child. Trying unsuccessfully to make rings, we watch the cigarette smoke eddy up and break on the wind. After discussing the relative merits of dogs versus cats, we start in on the conversation we always have: how we don't know what we'll do when we're out of this place.

The night tech comes out and finds us in serious conversation. He says he'll give us a few more minutes if we need it, and we nod solemnly. C tells me about FRED G, a process in which you write down your Fears, Resentments, moments of Ego, Deceptions, and what you're Grateful for.

"You've got to make the gratitude section just as important as the FRED part," she says.

"If we're supposed to make it just as important, then there should be at least four letters in the last part too," I reply—always the formalist. The night tech comes back and shoos us to bed. We've barely made it through Fears.

Later, I will forget nearly all of C's ambitions. I will remember only the clinical details: the disorders they diagnosed her with, the eager impotence of her sponsor. Nothing important.

C and I walk to a nearby coffee shop to use their computer that charges by the minute. There's a shortcut through an alley. We don't take shortcuts.

The neighborhood teens yell at us when we pass, "Sober house! Sober house!" A few days ago, some of the men my age from my halfway house, twenty-year-olds with something to prove, got in a scuffle with them. Now walking by these same teens, C stiffens, and I hope my smile appears jaunty. We keep going.

Then one night, it's after curfew, but C is nowhere to be found. In the basement of the halfway house, I talk about anything else nervously with other nervous people. Then my phone buzzes in my hand. The message says: *I'm sorry.*

"Probably crack," N says.

"Probably," I repeat.

C lies her way into a sober apartment, and I shuttle her from meeting to meeting in the weeks after her text. One afternoon, I sit with her and the two Zs. We sprawl on a knoll on the side of a road where cars always speed, and on the other side are the woods that lead down to the Mississippi. Peeking our heads up to look at the view, we take turns reading aloud from the Big Book of Alcoholics Anonymous and earnestly talk about how to forgive yourself.

One of the Zs isn't sure you can. The other thinks, if it's possible, it's all about spiritual fitness. I agree with both of them. C is silent.

———————

C slips again. And again. Again. Eventually, ashamedly, I purge her number from my phone. Later, my half-hearted searching will turn up empty.

AFTER CATULLUS

Since the world is foreign, it isn't mine. / Since you are en-tombed, it isn't yours. / Senseless fate split the you I remember / from the you that you were, / and all that remains ours is ritual.

THE THIRD AND FOURTH LESSONS

I am undone.

Isaiah 6:5

Galen is working on the script of a podcast about Søren Kierkegaard, whose work I read in college and didn't understand. Though the January snow has come and gone and left behind brittle ice, it is still a new year, so I decide to give Kierkegaard another chance. I pick up *Fear and Trembling*, his essay about Abraham and Isaac. I shiver on the porch, where I'm reading by the light through the kitchen windows. I make it halfway through the scholarly introduction before I turn to social media. A journalist whose work I respect says that she wants to kill the verb *to be*—wants to scrub it from her writing. I click the little heart button not because I dislike the verb *to be*, but because I recognize in her wish a brand of existentialism that appeals to me. I don't want *to be* either, but I can't help but keep living.

Still, bipolar disorder is boring. Or, terrifying, then boring. Or, alternated with days of an uncanny confidence and energy—a state my doctors call *hypomania*—then boring again. So I turn to Kierkegaard. Kierkegaard wonders at Abraham's ability to live inside a paradox: willing to sacrifice his son Isaac, able to love him all the same.

It has been eight years of continuous sobriety, and I am waiting to be licensed as a foster parent. Sober or no, guilt consumes me: I am so selfish as to want to take responsibility for a child when I can't even drive myself home after the doctor because we discussed the possibility of electroconvulsive therapy, and I was left bawling in my car. The paradox of mental illness is that it is at once mine and not, me and not.

This is true: I don't want *to be*.

This is also true: I don't want *to die*.

I don't undergo electroconvulsive therapy. Instead, a nurse wipes my arm with rubbing alcohol while I sit in a plush, reclinable armchair. He tells me there will be a little pinch, jabs a needle into my arm, and pumps me full of ketamine. I hate it. I apologize to him for hating it. I ask him to call Galen because I cannot move my arms properly—they are five sizes too big, and I am floating away, and though I can grasp at the lines of *Actus tragicus*, which I listen to on their noise-canceling headphones, not one will hold me down.

It's fine. I'm fine. Six infusions later, I am not afraid, though I would still not call the experience pleasurable.

I watch video after video describing the best way to get a baby to fall asleep, and the instructor says, "Mamas, you know what *that's* like." And while I am not a mama, and while I find the tone irksome, I already know what it's like to sleep only when a baby sleeps, to have my room awash in beach sounds, in perpetual twilight. I relate.

An acquaintance writes, *How can God exist if there's so much suffering?* This isn't a rhetorical question, he insists. He wants answers. Another acquaintance writes, beneath this, *I relate*, as though the experience of asking, and not the answer, is what's important. Today I agree with both my acquaintances. I click *like* beneath the struggle with the problem of evil. A faithful atheist, a recovering alcoholic, a self who has changed. The thing about a paradox, I suppose, is that you don't find your way out; you live inside it.

A long, long time ago, Plutarch wrote about the ship of Theseus, a ship that the Athenians wanted to commemorate and, over the course of many years, replaced bits and pieces of until nothing remained of the original. Later, much later, Roland Barthes would confuse Theseus's ship with the Argo—a different mythological boat—and, a bit later, Maggie Nelson would use the Argo as the titular metaphor of her book *The Argonauts*, leading the writer Melissa Mesku to wonder, cheekily: *Is a paradox still the same after its parts have been replaced?*

Today, just today, it's been nine years of continuous sobriety. The baby has started clapping (though not very well) in context, vocalizing her glee when Galen and I walk down to the tidal river mouth, ice spat up on the rocky shore by some mystery of the moon. The baby changes. Every day, a new skill. I am almost ashamed of how moving I find the banal growth of a child. But she doesn't worry if she's the same person, the same ship, the same paradox. This must be what those annoying, well-meaning parents mean when they talk about seeing with baby's eyes. I do, in fact, grudgingly, relate.

On my school's January break, I take off on an assignment from the college magazine, writing about young Christians in Colorado Springs. A day and a half into the three-day drive, I discover that boredom is physical: an ache in my left buttock, a knot in my right shoulder. At night, I read poetry while I eat undercooked pizza in the diner attached to a roadside motel. Rita Dove: *Halfway there the unknown but terribly / important essayist yelled Stop! / I wanna be in this; and walked / fifteen yards onto the land / before sky bore down and he came running / crying Jesus—there's nothing out there!* I look up at the cold image of my face in the curved silver of the napkin dispenser, and I don't know what lurks beneath this likeness, what invisible force joins this image of me to me. Recently, scientists snapped a picture of a point from which light cannot escape. I can't look away from this image of an unseeable thing. The apostle Paul to the Colossians: *Christ is the image of the invisible God.*

At a gas station, I walk out to the uneven field of gray pebbles and look through my camera at the endless, wild nothing because I want to be *in* this, but I can't bear to be. I snap a picture. I walk back to the gas station where I can see my bent reflection in the car's chrome. That night, I know, I will drink my way through the half bottle of gin in my backpack. John Calvin, glossing the apostle Paul to the Colossians: *God is invisible—not only to the eyes, but also to the understandings of men. He is revealed to us in Christ alone, that we may behold him as in a mirror.* Jesus, there's nothing out there.

When I stumble out of my car at a motel in Colorado Springs, I go straight to the bathroom. In the mirror, I see my beard has gnarled around my throat. I decide I will not drink again this trip.

But the view from my motel window is incredible. I don't believe it. Rivulets of gesso drip from the peak of the papier-mâché mountain; cotton-ball clouds jerk on a drawstring across the crayon-blue sky. I pour another finger into the cup and toss it back.

I sit in a youth pastor's office and try to make sense. He doesn't seem to understand my questions. He doesn't seem to understand me. I drive to more interviews with youth pastors. I drive to services on off days to hear sermons with audiovisual aids. I drive to a megachurch, take a tour, and worry the entire time that I stink of cigarettes. I drive along the broad streets that curve and loop back on each other and get lost all the time. The cardboard homes that line these roads all look the same. In my car's speakers, the music I used to love sounds tinny while the life-size diorama of things that ought to be beautiful flakes all around me.

I don't sing along at the church that offers new life. When I came here last week, I took notes. Now I sit in the back and just listen. Toward the end, they call forward those who want prayers. I step into the red-carpeted aisle and walk past rows of raised hands and closed eyes, and then I am before a man.

"I can't stop drinking," I whisper.

He leans in close, his breath on my cheek. "Are you ready to put yourself in God's hands?"

"Yes," I say.

"Tell Jesus that you need him here with you." His aftershave is caught in my nose, in my mouth, and I want to pull away, but I don't. Instead, I tell Jesus that I need him in my life. The man whispers something, his voice hoarse, but I can't make out the words because he's putting oil in the shape of a cross on my forehead, and where he touches me, I feel nothing but burning. I realize that tears are running from my eyes, and my chest is heaving. He smiles, and I smile back.

Back at the motel, the night dabs clouds on the dark canvas while I fix a drink. I reread my favorite psalm. *My enemies say to me all day long, "Where is your God?"* I used to hear the voice of the psalmist, feel the truth of it like I could live inside of it; now it's the facade of a poem, just like Pikes Peak is a cutout of a mountain. *My enemies say to me all day long, "Where is your suspension of disbelief?"*

I visit Pueblo, where a friend from school is staying with her family. Over dinner, her father details the infrastructure problems in this part of Colorado. From what little I can grasp, the utilities struggle to keep pace with the speed of construction. There's something about the particularities of the landscape that impact how they treat wastewater. I nod along, not really understanding, but envying his relationship with this place: where I see a toy town, he sees pipes, power, and shit.

After dinner, my friend and I drink 40s and take shots in a parking lot before going to dance next to men with ten-gallon hats. The slide guitar twangs behind my left eye. I am not having fun; I am having the idea of fun. I don't remember what happens next.

I come back to myself, my head still buzzing. I make my way to the shoulder, pull down the rearview, and look at my face, alternating red and blue, the taste of pennies in my mouth. My friend hums next to me, nervous.

"I'm sorry officer, I'm not from around here," I say. "I didn't realize you couldn't turn at this light." He leans his face in through the window, and I smell his breath. Like three old crones, knitting.

"*Nothing vast enters the lives of mortals without ruin,*" he says. A four-car pileup dances in his eyes. Wine seeps red through the snow. He sends us on our way. On the way back to school, somewhere in Nebraska, my car breaks down. I shave off my beard, shaken by what could have happened, what didn't happen.

A snowstorm comes. Little plows cut tracks atop the paths through the fields, and I walk in these canyons with my friends, passing bottles between us. As I drink, time becomes fluty, like sound caught by the wind over water. We are in someone's house. We are walking again. We are in a basement singing loudly. We are walking again. Then, I am lying in a snowbank, wearing only a T-shirt and jeans, and the gin has wrapped its arms around me.

The school administration requests that I meet with a doctor. Her face contorts with sympathy when I tell her that I'm just feeling sad these days. But I don't want her sympathy. She tells me about a meeting for people who can't stop drinking.

I am early to the small room in the bright Tudor building. The men give me warm looks. The chairs drawn up in a circle, the afternoon sun cutting sharp lines into the golden wood, I make myself small. *We will not regret the past nor wish to shut the door on it*, someone reads. I gasp. Psalm 42: *All your waves and breakers have swept over me*.

That night, I drink a pitcher of beer at the on-campus bar.

There's a picture of me taking a shot while Sam kisses my cheek. We are both blushing. I don't recognize this blushing boy. His youth. His full head of hair. Ready to die rather than change.

Coward.

The temptation of the mirror is that there's order on its surface, which is, in turn, the temptation of our lives—that there's order out there. In my dorm's bathroom, I decide that there is no order, save for what we give it. The break of a page. The beat of a cantata. The meter of a poem. Prayer. The soprano's voice arcs across the empty blue sky as it bears down, imploring *I wanna be* in *this*. There is no order, but there must be something out there.

My apartment is convenient to no one, but tonight, nearly all my friends trekked through slush to be here. We count it up, and, at this Christmas service, half of us are Jewish. I roast a ham and cook wild rice and we gorge on ice cream and hot fudge for dessert. I bake bread, and we take a secular communion. Gabe pounds his broad chest when we sing "Good King Wenceslas," and I am transported back to that first time we did this, but the memory is soft, like paper that's been folded over and over again.

We end with a reading from John: *And the Word became flesh and dwelt among us.*

Hardscrabble winter, gray and lonely, requires Christmas. Or, rather, in its depths, I require Christmas: words no longer cold, chrome, and barren, but alive, golden, cradled in my arms.

CAROL

For the Zs

They come and go together, their names—the same name—
one after the other on the sign-in/sign-out sheet. The Zs,
we say. They are both in their early twenties, birthdays in
the same month.

The three of us play chess. One is better than me. One is
worse. I won't remember any specific game, any particular
move, anything we talked about.

They claim to have slept with the same woman, an assistant who works at our halfway house. One after another, the same day, the same hour, they say. It's easy to imagine the cramped room, the low ceilings, the empty walls, the cold, sterile light reflecting off the bent, white plastic blinds, taking a moment of fleeting pleasure in doing something forbidden.

"Don't be a prude," one scolds.

"It's just sex," the other declares.

I don't believe them, but I recognize the species of pride they've pinned to their faces, a dead insect on cardboard, stiff, dry wings that would fall off if touched. Pride like this doesn't come from doing what you want, but from doing what you're not supposed to. I don't know the assistant well, but I doubt she wants this to become the gossip of the day, so I am repulsed by their breathless tone.

But I, too, understand the need to affix a label to your pain, inscribe its Latin name on a plaque. I don't know what to say, so I say nothing and feel like a coward when I start to avoid them.

One night, N tells me the Zs are coming down from crack. I talk with them before they are kicked out and let my imagination fill in the blanks: those days of high spring, everything is fraught with metaphors of rebirth. They climbed down where the Saint Paul High Bridge spans the river, above the flats on either bank, above the steep ridges— wooded, dark, and savage.

In high school, I spent nights pacing that bridge. Ignorant of what could be happening beneath, I took adolescent photos of the skyline, of the abandoned prison on the east flat, of the power plant to the south.

But the Zs wouldn't have seen this view—only the concrete columns, the wild forest, and the rushing river. Where or from whom they scored, I don't know, but they would have been flushed and excited. They would have walked in silence, quickly and with purpose, until they found a clearing somewhere on the west bank. They would have sat, muscles clenched in anticipation, brows furrowed, blood percussive in their ears. The tension would have risen, the dissonance of desire and doubt ringing in the air. Then the release.

I call the Z whose number I have after a release party for a book I know they would like at my favorite bookstore, and the phone rings and rings. I pull it away from my face. Robert Hass: *Longing, we say, because desire is full / of endless distances.* I put it back. It is still ringing. It might ring forever if I don't hang up.

AFTER CATULLUS

This is not my world that I travel on the way to your tomb to speak to dust. Fate gave you to me then took you from me, and all it left me was ritual.

THE FIFTH LESSON

Fear not.

Luke 1:30

On my porch, I watch the sun rise while the sound of white noise from the baby monitor statics in and out like surf on a beach. I have noticed sunrises before. I have noticed the robins that peck into our shaggy grass. I have noticed the little blue flowers whose names I don't know that grow cylindrical and weedy by the pale lilac bush. But I think that staring into the weeks-old baby's face, studying every twitch and grimace like it holds a secret, makes me more practiced in the art of noticing. Or maybe my lack of sleep has finally moved me beyond mere exhaustion, and into delirium.

I pull up Genesis and read the parts of the first chapters in which things are named for the first time. I want to name the little blue flowers. They already have a name; I just don't know it. The light is called *sun*, and it is good. It breaks over my neighbor's roof like a baby latching, finally, to her mother's nipple. It glints off the flowers whose name I just found. *Grape hyacinth*, I say, bringing them into focus at last.

I hold the baby at the hospital and am nearly sick with the thought that I could hold her wrong or drop her. I ask a nurse if the baby will die if I forget to burp her. She laughs at my question.

A friend says I should sleep when the baby sleeps, but every time I close my eyes, I imagine hitting her head on the door post, and her falling silent and dead in my arms, a trickle of black blood worming from her left nostril. I imagine not noticing a piece of fabric from her swaddle that has gotten loose and wrapped, snakelike, around her nose and mouth, and her face now the color of a bruise. I imagine tripping on the cat while rushing her from room to room, and not protecting her well enough when I fall, and her body lying twisted on the ground.

She screams into my face for almost an hour while I rock her and *shh* percussively. While I change her diaper. While I replace the pacifier again and again. Nothing helps. I have been crying, but now I am sobbing, and I try to close the door, but Galen hears me, and she takes the baby while I cry on the bed. Now I resent the sudden absence of wails. Galen's success. Fear and love knot together. When I pull on one, I tighten the other.

Then the baby's thumb catches on her sleeve, and she screams, sharp and clear, and I gasp. Then she will not sleep, and I stroke her head and wish I were someone else. Then one day, after four changes and feeds in a row, I ask Galen why I'm broken, why—tired, inadequate—I'm crying and she's not.

"You're not broken," she says. But I can't stop crying.

Figuratively, land is only ever dry when you've been on the water for too long. *It's only been two days*, I remind myself. *It's only been three days*, I say. *It's only been a week*, I say now.

I call her all sorts of things, because we don't know her name. *Baby*, I say. *Sweet Girl*, I say. *Yes, I hear you, Sweet Baby Girl*, I say. *Please stop crying, Little One*, I say. *You've shit in my hand, Dearest Darling Poopmonster.* Her soft, smooth poop smears across my palm while I—not quickly enough—put a fresh diaper underneath her. The land looks very dry. But I'm not ready to be put ashore.

My back is to the sun and the tall fence in the backyard of the halfway house. The metal patio tables shine as light glints off the glass of the door. N mistook a *Harry Potter* fanfiction (book-length) for an advance copy of the real McCoy. One of the Zs ribs him. I laugh easily. A month through my stay here, I feel like an old-timer. The door opens, and a new woman a few years older than me comes out. Her black hair—is it dyed?—sweeps to the side, asymmetrical. Wariness lurks behind her curious smile. I know this is her first day. Her name is A.

One night, N comes home with the newish M.I.A. CD. We decide to hold an impromptu dance party in the dining area. We use the sad, out-of-tune piano as a stand for the little stereo. We crank the volume knob up. Tinny sound washes over the room. A runs her hand through her choppy haircut, and it sticks up in all directions. Her bangs remain resolutely plastered to her forehead. I point at her hair, grinning, and she laughs and musses it up even more. N and the two Zs are drinking glass after glass of milk from the dispenser. They eat bread smothered with butter, sugar, and cinnamon, laughing.

At a copy shop in Saint Paul, I write *FOR A* on the cover of a book of poems I didn't write. The cheap glue I use to attach the cover bleeds out onto my hands, where it will stay for days. A loves it. We celebrate by going to a young people's meeting.

"This is not a meeting where you get solution," I say after.

"This is a meeting where you pick up chicks," A agrees.

The neighborhood with the halfway home is littered with sober living apartments. When we graduate, A and I both find rooms within two blocks of the old house. She has a porch, and her roommates grow accustomed to finding us there talking in low voices in green plastic lawn chairs.

I work for a woman with a brassy voice at a coffee shop that's nearly always empty. I am the night shift manager, which mostly means I clean up after we close. A comes by one night just before closing, and I make the most complicated espresso drinks I can. No one else is here, so I abandon my post, and we go outside to smoke.

It is summer. Feeling the joy of it, I put on "Summertime" from *Porgy and Bess*, the music spilling out from the doors I propped open. Louis Armstrong plays three notes fit to burst. I could burst.

I get up at 8 a.m. on Saturday to make coffee in my surprisingly spacious kitchen. I smoke a cigarette outside while I wait for the scratched Mr. Coffee to finish brewing. In one travel mug, I drop two ice cubes. In the other, I mix in milk.

I pick A up in my car. She smiles at the travel mug with milk, raising it to her lips. We don't talk. When we arrive downtown, twenty minutes later, we park the car and she feeds the meter. We go up a flight of stairs. The glassy, wooden floor of the dance studio gleams in the early-morning air. We greet the others and warm up, then put our bodies to use in a run of complicated choreography that leaves me winded.

I want to live inside my body. I want to feel myself in every crevice of it. In the stretch marks on my belly—two on either side, at 45-degree angles, slashing down toward my crotch. In the wiry, thick black hairs on my upper back and shoulders. In my chapped lips. A lives in her body, I know. I see it when she stretches, bending into a curve over her legs, sighing with pleasure. Envy and awe fill me in equal measure. The instructor asks if we're a couple. I smile with my teeth. A answers. "No," she says. "We're best friends."

A and I go to my favorite meeting. I try to ignore that it's in my parents' neighborhood. After, we go to a coffee shop I frequented in high school.

"It used to be," she confides, "that I was A with speed. Now I'm A with AA, but I want to be just A."

I try to say something comforting, but I, too, am not sure about this bargain we've each made—life at the cost of total change.

A flakes on me twice in a row, and I show up, unannounced, to the pet store where she works. She smiles a strange smile; it is not her smile.

That night, in a fit of nostalgia, I go to a late showing of a movie—a Korean thriller about a monster—at the Uptown Theatre with some friends from high school. A texts halfway through the movie. The monster is rampaging, killing, out of control. She says she needs some space. It wasn't OK that I showed up at her work. I text back an acknowledgment and am glad no one can see me cry.

The poet Robert Lowell left his second wife, Elizabeth Hardwick, and their daughter for a younger woman. He took the letters Hardwick wrote him, begging him to come back, changed a few words, enjambed them, and published them in his book *The Dolphin*. "The Dolphin" was his nickname for his third wife.

Elizabeth Bishop, appalled, scolded Lowell in a letter: *But art just isn't worth that much*. I know art isn't worth that much, but sometimes, I envy Lowell's willingness to give everything up, even human decency, to whatever strange version of art he believed in—to a cause greater than himself. I sometimes fear we're almost the same, though I'm no poet: two men, minds aflame, alone in private clearings of charred twigs, ash adrift on the air, wondering where the birds all went.

A and I reconcile. We drive back from a cabin in Wisconsin—a little weekend jaunt. We laugh and listen to Nina Simone in the car. We drink 8 p.m. espresso at a shop where Chairman Mao wears Mickey Mouse ears. Then, sitting side by side on the porch of her sober house in green, plastic lawn chairs, we talk about each other, about us.

"I can't give you any more," she says. I don't look at her face directly; I look at its reflection in the window. The thick white paint on the sill peels with imperceptible slowness while she reads me a poem she wrote about birds. It is beautiful, and I'm struck, suddenly, by the truth of this moment. It's true that we're best friends. It's true that her poem is beautiful. But though Keats said some wild shit about *beauty* and *truth*, we know better. Neither one requires the other, and even if *beauty is truth, truth beauty*, well, *art just isn't worth that much*.

A wants to be *just A*—the true A. I want to be the true *me* too, I suppose. But Keats wasn't all wrong. It's better to say that truth, not beauty, is in the eye of the beholder. It's better to say that beauty, not truth, will out. If you work for it.

A and I are on the west side of the road where cars always speed. On the east side, the trees that screen the Mississippi eat the light from the cars. She takes my hand, and we run across the street. The trees bite our clothes as we climb down to the river. I feel like we're on a pilgrimage. We are probably just bored. The halfway house and sober homes are a world away once you can't see the lights of the street, which is the way we want it. Between the mosquitoes and the cuts and the otherworldly concrete pillars, choked with vines, we don't make it down to the riverbank. We turn back. At the house, away from the sound of rushing water, away from the shadow of the bridge, we sit together and watch the man with the lawnmower make the dusky air smell like summer.

"But I didn't take your hand," A protests.

I decide to go back to school, but before I do, I return A's box set of *Star Trek: Deep Space Nine* and her yoga workout video. I leave. Our contact goes from a torrent to a trickle. Then it stops. There's a picture of me and A, arms wrapped around each other, both laughing, my face raised, hers lowered. We will never see each other again.

Winter in Chicago comes stealthily. I wake up and find the bright long days smothered in snow. I am at the gym down the block from our apartment one night, marveling at the blizzard, when a plow drives by, heaping feet of snow onto the curb.

The man next to me points out the window and laughs. "Whoever drives that Prius is gonna have a bitch of time getting out," he says.

I look out and laugh too. It's only after I leave that I realize it's our Prius. Galen and I spend an hour shoveling through the slush.

"God can move mountains; just bring a shovel," V tells me.

This year, I want to make my Lessons and Carols a joint production—mine and Galen's. We lay out the text and send it to a professional printer. We invite all our Chicago friends, and Galen makes a complicated chickpea dish for the vegetarians. I am silent and smiling, but apparently I have written on my face that *chickpeas are not for Christmas.* Galen rolls her eyes and keeps cooking. This is a work in progress.

Flights are cheap, so Sonia flies to Chicago for my Lessons and Carols. We sit on the floor of my living room and sew the Coptic-bound books for this year's party. One winter, up in rural Wisconsin, before so many friendships fell off their boughs and turned to mulch for new ones, I caught Sonia in front of the fire, rocking back and forth with a blanket over her shoulders, mouthing the words to "Silent Night" and weeping. She loves Christmas maybe as much as I do—and maybe even in the same way.

I worry, though, that the *real* version of me is almost certainly a *sad* version of me. I worry that the *real* version of me is not the *best* version of me.

CAROL

For the boy whose name I forgot

On a summer break from college, I walk around the lake near my parents' home, in the center of Minneapolis. Bikes whiz by on the upper path. Down here, breathless runners pass me going both ways. B tells me that a boy we knew from rehab is dead.

Here is the almost-complete list of things I remember about this boy: (1) He had a hole in his heart. (2) In rehab, he and I sat in the thin concrete courtyard with the sad plants. I had bought a pack of foul, sweet, pink-detailed cigarettes from my roommate, and this boy was scornful as he handed me a Camel Light. (3) He was partial to a mix of cocaine and heroin. The word he used was *speedball*. I had to ask what that was, and he laughed incredulously. (4) I learned what Suboxone was—a drug to block the brain's opioid receptors—from him the day his body began to shake and he was whisked away. (5) He was wearing khaki pants and a thin, soft T-shirt. Maybe lime green or pastel pink or powder blue—all he ever wore. (6) He borrowed a book from me and never returned it. I remember the book. I do not, now, remember his name.

I sit down on a bench marked with names—tags etched deep into the dark gray wood. I pick down in the grooves, furious. He knew his heart was weak. He is the first I know to die.

The break from school feels interminable. I keep myself busy by remembering everything I can about the dead boy, which isn't much—isn't enough. I buy a new copy of the book I never got back. I try to reread it. I can't.

In learning a language, there is the moment when you know the word *to clean*. Then maybe you learn *to sweep* or *to polish* or *to scrub*. There is a moment after that too, Galen and I decide, when you know all the words, and still are unable to represent with perfect fidelity the concept you want to share. Robert Hass: *Because there is in this world no one thing / to which the bramble of* blackberry *corresponds, / a word is elegy to what it signifies.*

I am talking about addiction and death with V. As we make our slow, irregular orbit of the streets outside the just-closed coffee shop, I note silently that Hass's poem is mine too. I hear my disbelief and anger that all my memories cannot translate the dead back to something I recognize as human—as something not uncanny and foreign.

AFTER CATULLUS

The world is a feral dog on a chain. You think you know it, but then it shows its teeth and growls when you walk by on your way to the bright corner café where you want to sit outside and read Catullus.

Catullus does not speak to me, *I think, now that I'm at the coffee shop. I can't get my own voice out of the way. I sit, instead, and wonder at the senselessness of it—that rickety ritual is the only bridge I have that crosses to the past.*

THE SIXTH LESSON

Each went to their own place.

Luke 2:3

Our cat is angry. I can't say I blame her. We don't let her come into the bedroom while we sleep, even though it doesn't seem particularly likely that she could get into the baby's crib and kill a newborn. She's a small cat, only eight or nine pounds, but next to the baby, a shade over six pounds, she looks fierce and wild.

We named our cat Geryon, like the monster in Greek mythology whom Herakles slays. She is less like a monster, though, than like the boy in Anne Carson's book reimagining the myth. By this, I mean she is meek and full of noticing. But what can you really notice absent language? While I angle the bottle at 45 degrees like the nurse taught me, I watch Geryon stare at the shadows from the pine tree that pass through the gauzy linen curtains in our bedroom. I notice her noticing them, seeing the abstract shapes that my brain wants to make into concrete ones. Then Geryon notices the smell of the baby, and she sniffs the baby's thin, already-curly hair while I try to use my knee to keep the beast at bay.

"Should we bottle-feed you, Geryon?" Galen asks, swooping down, gathering the cat's tense body in her arms. "Look, now we're each holding a baby."

I have more important things to do than rock a baby to sleep, so I am grumpy when she bursts her arms free of the swaddle, startles herself, and cries. I am annoyed when she spits her pacifier out, again and again, when all I want to do is go read a book on the porch with my morning coffee. I grumble rude things when she will not go back to sleep and wants only to let me know her displeasure.

"What do you want, baby?"

She doesn't answer.

I dress her in her little lamb outfit. Tiny lamb-socks for her feet. Small sheep on her shirt. Warm wool sweater. What she wants, after I've fed and burped her, after I've put the pacifier in her mouth, after I've rocked her until her eyes are closed, remains a mystery. But I herd her back to sleep again and again.

She's been in our house for a time measured in weeks, but already I've gleaned that parenting is a constant state, and it's in the process, rather than in the grand moments, that I'll need to find joy. I sometimes do. More and more.

Between the baby in my home and the baby in these pages, there is a connection. But never be confused. One I love because she is herself. But if I love the other, then I fear that I am gazing soppily into a pond, wasting away, Narcissus with a keyboard.

My off-campus apartment is never warm enough, but I can't bring myself to care. I am failing classes. I am failing my friends. I am failing all the external markers of success save one: I have not had a drink in four years. At my desk, I take in a quick breath, then I stub a cigarette out on my wrist. I whimper but I am determined to hold it in place. It leaves a scar. Sobbing, I call R. He comes over, and he convinces me to call my mom. She flies down and, for the second time in my life, checks me into a hospital.

After I leave, a friend says that I should write about it.

"You must have met some real characters in there," he says.

"Not really," I say. "Mostly just sad, frightened people."

In January, everyone has gone to big cities to do big projects, and I'm left in my college town. I'm sitting on the battered recliner that smells like wet dog, and I have a bag of frozen, miniature candy bars, that I alternate with long drafts of whole milk. Last year, I read Michael Pollan. The whole milk is a concession to him. Less processed, I tell myself. It justifies the candy bars. I am reading by the half-broken radiator, hunched under a garish blanket that I stole from Ellen.

In my combined living and dining room, the wall is cramped with art, framed and unframed, their edges aristocratically close together. Across the room, against the wall paneled in fake wood, is the bench I made, cut from two-by-fours and plywood, covered in a bedsheet and pillows. Enrico's cherrywood table sits behind me, in the center of the room.

"What kind of wood?" Enrico had asked me.

"Pine," I had said.

"I got you cherry," he told me when he got back from the lumberyard. We were standing in the woodshop, gleaming silver machines all around us. He ripped a long strip off one of the new boards.

"Smell it," he said. I smelled it: a lone cherry tree ablaze, set on a green field, black smoke billowing up like in a movie.

The empty folding chairs sit around the table. There is a desk. There is a wall full of books, shelves I put up.

Enrico came over with a chalk line and a stud finder.

"I found a stud," I exclaimed, holding the device over his abdomen. He raised his eyebrows and didn't laugh. We snapped the string of the chalk line against the wall, and it made a satisfying report. A faint, powdery mist filled the air and then disappeared like in a magic trick. Enrico showed me how to mount the brackets in the wall, black brackets, mostly hidden from sight once the unvarnished poplar boards were screwed in—the wood creamy with streaks of purple and green snaking through it like veins. I did the joke with the stud finder again. This time he laughed. Otis Redding crooned from the big computer on the desk.

The light in my apartment is timid. Two windows. One by the door, half-sized at best, is covered by a yellow curtain that was once white. The other, long window with inexplicably frosted glass sits above the radiator, looking out on the backyard choked with strange scraggly bushes. Snow is building up on their spindly branches, pooling in a patch of ground I cleared for my failed garden. There were carrots there once, which the local animals enjoyed before I abandoned the enterprise. Flowers and weeds are all that survived.

I am supposed to be learning yoga for my January term, but I withdrew a few days into the class. I started crying during child's pose. I left embarrassed. The teacher tells me that this can happen sometimes, that some poses can pull emotions out of you that you forgot you had.

I want my friends to come back to this tiny town where everything is closer to all right than anywhere before. I don't want to be sad anymore. But I don't even know what happy looks like. Anne Carson notes that *cliché*, a French loan word, comes from the sounds of old copy machines when they make an impression. A whole existence full of fading simulacra of loneliness, misregistered blueprints for a life.

And then, suddenly, my friends come back to campus. And then it is the day before Valentine's Day. On the street of this small college town, just in front of the local bar, I run into a person I dislike.

"Hey," he says. "How about a drink? I'd love to pick your brain."

"Sure," I say. *I'll just get a ginger ale*, I think.

I order, instead, a glass of Laphroaig.

The bartender pours me a double. It sits in front of me, and I am so very tired. Tired of doing the next right thing. Tired of being in this stifling town. I drink it straight. I drink another. I stop counting how many fingers I've drunk. I think about what I am doing—play the tape forward to its inevitable end—and I find I do not care that it will cause pain to me, to my friends, to my family. Later, LC will tell me that they can forgive everything except cruelty, except taking pleasure in causing pain. The secret to drinking a lot is sociopathy, I sometimes think.

I go to the general store and buy a bottle of clear liquid that purports to be vodka. I bring it home. Gabe is coming over soon to work on a website with me. I pour a water glass full of vodka and think about my day. I am not sad yet, which surprises me. I am always sad when I drink—but thinking about my surprise might make me sad, so I stop thinking about that and focus on the blurry feeling in my brain. I will not think about regret. I will not think about this act of betrayal.

Gabe arrives, and I ask him if he would like a drink. He smiles unnaturally.

"I don't know what to do," he says.

"You should probably call R," I say with a sigh. He steps outside to make the call, and I am alone. The sadness takes me as I drink more. Then R arrives. He snatches up my drink. He pours out my handle. He brings me to his apartment, where I sleep. I awake hung over, a sensation I forgot.

Resentment pools within me. The current requires a concrete will to hold it back. I am the Hoover Dam. I am the Three Gorges. I resent so much, the public works project my river necessitates displaces the surrounding towns.

Enrico built me something solid and beautiful from something else solid and beautiful; it was only while under construction that it seemed flimsy. But I am not a table, though I often wish I were.

Galen extemporizes an introduction to our Lessons and Carols while I rush to check the ham in the oven. Condensation has formed on the windows, lengthening the orange glow from the lights that mark the bike path that snakes behind our apartment. I crack a window to keep the heat down a bit and, suddenly, the past rattles its tail. This is not the first time I've made ham in an inadequate oven, the first time I've opened a window to the December air. I know I ought to avoid resentment, but I'm almost in the mood to be reckless. Let this feeling bite my leg. I'll suck the poison out myself.

But I deny the resentment its chance to strike.

We don't have many friends yet in Boston, but here's Karim, in town for work, sitting on the ground with his back against the wall, offering to be a wise man. There's a new friend from the office, playing his violin with enough vibrato for the Romantic era on "O Little Town of Bethlehem." I've practiced on the small electric keyboard enough that I can really take in the words while I play. Phillips Brooks: *No ear may hear his coming, / but in this world of sin, / where meek souls will receive him, still / the dear Christ enters in.*

It's true that God walks softly, that no ear may hear him. It's so soft, I can't quite bring myself to believe in him. Sin fills this world so completely, it might split open. I almost want it to. I close my eyes because, it turns out, resentment can't be denied. It can only be deferred—or worked through.

John Calvin: *God is invisible—not only to the eyes, but also to the understandings of men. He is revealed to us in Christ alone, that we may behold him as in a mirror.*

Phillips Brooks: *No ear may hear his coming.*

I don't know what it would mean to feel only once—and not again and again. I don't know how something I can neither see nor hear could possibly save me.

A couple of friends stay with us. After the festivities and the feast, we set up an air mattress in the dining room, put sheets on the couch in the spare bedroom. Alone, I go downstairs, stand in the concrete courtyard, and light a cigarette. Cars pass by, but I don't see them, don't hear the sound of tires on salt. The door opens behind me, and David is there, smiling, framed in the fluorescent light that rushes through the doorway, pushing through the edges of his curly hair.

We smoke another cigarette while he gesticulates through a story about nothing and I am laughing and smiling with him. So, it is love, after all, that humbles me—the only surface that reflects the invisible divine. The only medium that transmits the sound of the spirit. Carefully, we stub out our cigarettes, toss them in the trash can. In bed, Galen and I curl into each other.

In the morning, I wake early, before the sun rises, careful not to wake the others. I mix two doughs, one for bagels and one for cinnamon buns. I let the bagel dough rise while I roll the buns. I bake the buns while I shape and boil the bagels. I pile the table with frosting and cream cheese, lox and capers. When everyone is awake, we eat. *Enter in*, I pray silently over the meal while my friends talk all around me, the meek sun low in the sky. *Please, enter in.*

CAROL

For N

I am lounging on my couch when a picture of N pops up on my phone. He stares out at me: a young man, my age, with unruly hair and a blasphemous, ratty shirt. The unknown poster captioned the photo *RIP*.

The last time we talked, we fought. I remained familiar with his life through profile pictures and status updates. He became a sober companion. He moved out west. He had girlfriends—so many of them!—and they looked just like him; I pictured the same cans of Rockstar clutched in their hands as they danced together in a dingy, rented-out church gymnasium. He had trouble staying sober.

His friends paste snippets of song lyrics and poems on his Facebook: death-gifts, what they have to offer.

When, all those years ago, I went to Colorado Springs to write about evangelical Christians and drink in peace, I knew my motel room's view of Pikes Peak was supposed to be awe-inspiring, but to me it appeared flimsy in the cold sun. I sat in the floral armchair that looked out the window. Defiant, I left the shades open, let the clouds cut shadows into the wall behind me while I stared back at the unreal mountain. I ran out of tonic and closed the shades before I poured a short glass of straight gin.

I wanted this, like every time, to be the last. I knew it wouldn't be. Before N shot up for the last time, did he know?

I tell Galen that I am writing about people who have died, writing that I don't understand why *them* and not *me*, and she gives me words—*survivor's guilt*. I want to reject these words. I, too, am dead. Or rather, I should be. I walk this world that is not mine; the me that knew N is dead, though *that* me still stands behind *this* me, a ghostly puppeteer, and moves my limbs.

I sometimes think that living takes great courage or a willingness to blind oneself to the inadequacies of our worldly knowledge. I have been paralyzed by skepticism—by core-shaking failures of communication, by language's inability to mean. So, how do I know that the world is real? G. E. Moore: *Here is one hand. And here is another.* How do I know that language can ever mean? *Here is one word. And here is another.*

AFTER CATULLUS

I follow you to the unfamiliar riverbank, where I am startled by each detail: / the willow's lank leaves, the unseen woodpecker's rattle, your absence. / ("It is so much like a beach after all," Ashbery wrote, "where you stand and think of going no further.") / You will go no further. / You're gone. I can't see the woodpecker. / But I say my stupid words in their stupid order. / This is brutal, senseless, useless. / Then, suddenly, the woodpecker flicks across my sight. / I want Dickinson to be right, that hope has feathers.

THE SEVENTH LESSON

What a thing: the wild strangeness of God.

Luke 2:19

I have read Genesis more times in the last week with the baby than in all the weeks preceding this one. I nestle in the covers, make a tent with my legs so that there's room for Geryon to curl up next to me beneath the blanket. I hold the baby in my arms and read, the light on my phone set all the way down. I have always been obsessed with the beginnings of things, the stories we tell about them. I've often lost interest after the beginnings, because that's when the work becomes visible. The burst of inspiration seems sacred. The work to execute it seems base. The baby fusses in my arms.

A friend says that in any couple with a baby, the one who didn't literally give birth is an adoptive parent. I can see the seams of this story we're making, feel myself willing love into existence. It wells up, like a miracle.

"God can move mountains; just bring a shovel," V tells me again.

I play the recorder for the baby while Galen feeds her, and she is so distracted that she spits up. David says we can't force a child to want to play music. I know he's right, but I miss the future where we play music together and immediately offer to take the baby from Galen so I can stare into her face and imagine what might come.

I want to teach her about music because I want her to know how fragile the concept of a piece is, by which I mean how fragile the concept of a self is. But fragility can be beautiful, if handled right.

Then again, a friend says babies are tougher than I give them credit for. I saw the way the nurses at the hospital held her, how they were neither rough nor gentle. Another friend says I should consider treating myself like a baby—that is, not with fragility, but with care. I think I want to treat myself with care. It's obviously not working, this heaving shame I feel when the baby does not fall asleep in my arms. Who am I without the name *unlovable*?

The morning after Galen and I were married, we took a selfie in a mirror, and I thought, *I am not concerned, at this moment, with the question of my own unlovability*. Marriage did not redeem me any more than this baby will redeem me. It did not cause me to feel loved. It caused me, for just a moment, not to obsess.

Someday, this baby will wonder, in all likelihood, if she is lovable. *Yes*, I want her to remember, *I am held and loved*. I want her to be like soft metal: neither rigid nor weak, but malleable, worked, and burnished in a rosy sun.

Surprise is the only thing that interrupts her cry while we rub soapy water on her body. We dab the wet washcloth onto her stomach, and her eyes go wide, and her mouth makes a little *o*, and her arms come down. Then we lift the washcloth, and her arms tremble and raise up above her head, and she wails once more.

"Can you get her pacifier?" Galen asks.

"I want to be able to hear what she does and doesn't like."

It turns out she doesn't like everything about this experience, so I get the pacifier and push it into her mouth. Overly optimistic, I set up my fancy camera to record this moment—baby's first sponge bath in our house!—and my phone is blaring "Beautiful Love" like a soundtrack. What surprises me about the gathering of waters on her chest is that I am aware of how mundane it is, aware of how messily physical this experience is, aware that not an hour earlier, I was bawling my eyes out because I thought, insanely, that she hated me. But I still see the numinous in this, the bass player taking a solo, the piano hitting the important changes. Like I'm in the corner of the room, watching *these* people take care of *this* baby, and each moment is bathed in a warm glow.

Shortly after graduation, I sit in the corner of my New York living room, in the deep sill of the window over the fire escape. My cane leans against the wall. I crawl my left leg up under me, but I keep my right leg—the one in a brace—out straight, rest it on a cheap ottoman, study the neighbor's roof, where pigeons roost. My neighbor feeds them from time to time out of a white plastic bucket, the kind you might use to compost. He climbs up the ladder and throws the seed out onto the flat roof, and the birds go nuts. When a car backfires, they flutter away as one. Ellen just called. She doesn't want me to come.

I am careful to blow the smoke out the window, turning my back toward the room. My cousin gave me five black chairs that sit around Enrico's cherrywood table. I don't use the desk. I hung art on the walls. I bought an uncomfortable blue couch. The sunlight is perfect in this apartment; every room has a window. In an effort to make the seed money last just a little while longer, the start-up I work for doesn't have an office anymore, so I've been working from home. My boss, the CTO, has just quit, and I have been made the interim CTO, which looks very good on my résumé. My knee has been repaired, but I'm still on a cane. Ellen is in her last year of college, three states away.

I decide that I will agree with Ellen. No, I should not get on a train to Ohio. No, it is not a good idea. Yes, we need to understand what we are to each other first. But the truth is that I'm in the mood to reach and grasp without looking. For too long, I've been trying to cast spells over the dirty bones of our relationship. I'd rather burn them brittle, grind them down to ash, fertilize the ground, make room for something new between us. This is magic of another sort, magical thinking. This is gardening. But Ellen is not soil for my wants.

I get a new job. I'm still a software engineer, but now in a sunny, pleasant office in an obnoxiously hip part of Manhattan. During the day, I make web ads for companies like Goldman Sachs. At night, I read Matt Taibbi's book on the financial crisis. He calls Goldman Sachs *a great vampire squid wrapped around the face of humanity, relentlessly jamming its blood funnel into anything that smells like money.* Capitalism makes companies into vampire squids, and it has people like me design web ads for them to pay the bills. This is what I tell myself. I look for new work, but not too hard. At night, on the subway, I read and reread Robert Lowell's "Skunk Hour" until I know it by memory. *My mind's not right.*

Maggie Nelson: *Loneliness is solitude with a problem.* Depression, I think, is frustration with nothing to do. Bipolar disorder is cardboard boredom punched through with terror. Light streams in through the holes. But I dislike the word *depression*. I dislike the words *bipolar disorder* even more. I sometimes wonder what would happen if I peeled off diagnosis, if it came away in long strips, ragged at the edges. Would I discover, within myself, something revelatory? Most likely, I'd flay myself for nothing.

I tell myself that I have a lot going for me. Though I've been younger, I am young still. I have been smarter, but I am smart still. My family loves me. My friends love me. I haven't had a drink in months. I arrange these facts in my journal on the pro side. Looking down, I am terribly sad. I see, at first, just an indistinct blackness, but then, as my brain catches the scale, I realize it is actually the caverns of a yawning maw. I want it to swallow me whole.

The pigeons rise in the air as a single entity. I have not left my apartment in days, weeks maybe, except to buy food and cigarettes at the corner store. The mailman has left a note.

The recycling bin is overflowing again. It seems to accuse me, the empty personal-size pizza boxes pushing out of its mouth like vomit. I tease off the bin's plastic lid, and I stack the boxes, one by one, on the counter by the stove. I take a picture of these boxes, as though I might laugh about it later. I am going to die in this apartment, and I don't even have a cat to gnaw on my bones. Ha ha.

My mom flies out. We write a list of things I absolutely must do: take my medication, shower, clean the house, leave the house, check my mail, pay my bills. I quit my job. Will this make me happy? It has been just over a year since the hospital. I am not happy yet.

I usher in the new year with a big box of Popeye's fried chicken and a high school rom-com. All our mutual friends have gone to hear the steam whistles at the Pratt Institute. It's a sound like no other, they tell me. But I'm still miserable, and my leg hurts all the time, so Karim and I sit together on my poorly assembled IKEA couch, and the light from the television casts his face in cold, flickering patterns.

In a fit of imaginative projection, Karim and I decide to buy cigars from the twenty-four-hour bodega on the corner. We pick our way down the broken Brooklyn sidewalk. With my cane, my gait is uneven and slow, and Karim takes small, quick steps next to me like a hobbled racehorse.

I have always wanted to be the kind of person who enjoys smoking cigars. One night, just after graduating high school, a friend and I climbed the hill in Prospect Park in Minneapolis with a bottle of scotch and smoked twenty dollars' worth looking out over the city, its downtown framed in the arch of a tree. I know I am trying to capture the past by enacting it in the present. What is the uncanny but the past, the familiar, in the mask of the present, a stranger?

Karim and I pass the kids who sit on their stoops even in snowy winter, and we nod to each other as we walk by. They talk to me every so often as I speed-limp to a train that I am sure to miss. One told me I'm just like Jeremy Lin, a basketball player with a bum knee. I was perhaps too excited that I understood the reference. When I told him that all I heard was a wet pop when I tore my ACL, he barked an infectious laugh.

I'm still sore, and the odd movement will spike pain through my leg, but as Karim and I talk about nothing on the way down the street in the last, crisp night of a year, I can almost ignore it. The bodega's hand-painted sign blares its bright lie: GOURMET FOOD.

We edge our way out onto the lip of the window that opens onto the fire escape. The black metal is rounded with ice. I imagine slipping on the ledge, my weakened knee not catching me, falling, falling into my neighbor's yard where they have summer cookouts. I do not say, "Karim, I am lonely." I do not say, "Karim, I am about to start another job I don't want, that feels wrong, writing code for a company I don't trust." I do not say, "Karim, I wish I were able to drink champagne until I stop remembering my own name."

Loneliness is so pretty in the distance you might mistake it for solitude. When the sun shines down and squirrels make their way outside, trunks glisten in the still, clear air. But ice storms fell trees.

"Karim," I say, "thank you for being here with me."

"Love you, bud."

Then we turn *Easy A* back on, and I watch Karim's face shift in strange shapes under the TV's unnatural glare.

Karim is asleep on my couch. Maybe we'll make pancakes in the morning.

I go on terrible OkCupid dates with terrible matches. The only good news is that I am not going on many of them. "You had more hair in your profile picture," one complains. This is accurate—my hairline recoils from my head as though it were scalding—so I laugh and say nothing. Later, we argue about the mentally ill. "I don't want to round them up or anything," she says. I get the check.

The date is at the restaurant where Alice works, in an upscale neighborhood in Brooklyn. I find myself spending weekends there. The food is good, and the coffee is passable, and the neighborhood is pleasant and bright. When my date leaves, Alice swings over and sits.

"That seemed to go well," she says.

"Did you hear what she said?"

"Of course not."

I tell her.

"How did you even get talking about that?" she asks.

"We were talking about the Newtown shootings."

"Oh," Alice laughs, "so it was already going really well."

It is Valentine's Day, and I go speed dating at Alice's bar. I have been sober again for exactly one year, but I do not say this to the woman with the faint New Jersey accent who sits across from me. Later, we go on a walk in Prospect Park, and I am happy because I no longer have a cane. I ask if I can kiss her, and she says yes.

Alice has been seeing this woman's roommate, who is funny. I walk, cane-less, carefree—I am so fast now!—to their basement apartment. Alice is on her way, but for a moment, I am alone with my date and her roommate and their friends, almost all of whom want to be comedians. Jokes, impressions, hysterics in rising tones. Then Alice arrives, and I am saved from further experiments in humor.

My date turns off her phone before we eat dinner, and I find this endlessly endearing. Later, I tell Karim about her sly accent, her turned-off phone, and he tells me that I need to flirt better. He tells me to play it cool. But I never learned to flirt sober—or really at all—and playing it cool when I am not feels like a lie. So, I spend too much money on tickets to Benjamin Britten's *The Turn of the Screw* at the Brooklyn Academy of Music. I call her but she doesn't answer. Then Alice tells me that she told her while they were drunk that she thinks I am more into her than she is into me. I tell Alice that I would appreciate it if it came from her, and not through a game of drunken telephone. Alice says that this is selfish. I do not think this is selfish. Alice says that I am selfish because in this patriarchal world, why would I demand that she reject a man's desire in person?

After Alice tells me this, I go to a Starbucks bathroom to be alone, and I think of questions to put to her. I want to stay indignant, but, then again, all I can think of are the times when I tried on, like an ill-fitting shirt, my desire to be desired. As a teenager, I vomited in a club bathroom rather than wear it for long. I took my glasses off, put them on the sink, and in the mirror, my pale, young face was drained of color atop the pink blur of my sweater. I had come here to get on my knees and suck some boy off, though I didn't go through with it. Perhaps my mere gaze can inflict—and since when do men only gaze, anyway?

I don't speak with my date again. The truth is, I am relieved.

The truth is, it's easier to be heartbroken by Ellen than to be heartbroken by someone new.

Emily Dickinson: *"Hope" is the thing with feathers.* Also Emily Dickinson: *A great Hope fell / You heard no noise.* Question for Emily: Is hope a pigeon taking flight or a felled tree?

Ellen comes to New York. We eat at my favorite restaurant in all of Brooklyn. We are sitting outside, in their quiet backyard, under a twinkle light–strewn tree. Ellen and I whisper-yell over my steak and ginger ale, taking turns crying. I vow to never go back there again. I rage-smoke a cigarette looking out at the traffic on Atlantic Avenue, and know I should apologize, but I don't. I will not remember the content of the fight, only that we fought.

She comes out eventually and says she's worried about me. She thinks my apartment is messy. This is code for she thinks my life is messy, that I am not handling my depression correctly. I silently protest. *I am sober. I am employed. I have everything except you.*

David, Alice, and I will be at a cabin in the woods before we know it. Vacation is what I need—perhaps all I need, if I can convince Ellen to come. David and I will take his battered PT Cruiser from Brooklyn to Ohio, where we will see Ellen graduate. Then we will drive to Chicago and pick up Alice, who wisely left New York. Then we will drive all the way to Wisconsin and stay there for three days. We will drive back, drop off Alice, spend one more night in Ohio. Then back to New York. David plans to bring his girlfriend. Alice plans to bring her boyfriend. I plan to bring Ellen. None of these others will come.

In Ohio, my friends crash with Ellen. Not I. "Do you think that would be a good idea?" she asks, rhetorically, gently.

We take a picture together. Why are there no pictures of us together when we were together? When did we make that decision: no pictures? I told Karim that I wanted to see her get her diploma—wanted to cheer and shout until I was hoarse. She did the same for me, I said. She walks by us in her red dress. I snap a picture, her defiant stance, a diploma in one hand, her middle finger extended in the other—laughing.

The day of Ellen's graduation, I walk all around campus. Here is my apartment. Here is where my mom flew out and checked me into the hospital.

David and I drive on, and I make him pull over so I can cry. I ask him to let me drive, and I take the car along the thin, straight strip of road, like a ripped piece of shirt, in the dark pine forest. We never took pictures. We never took a vacation. I don't know which is sadder. They are the same problem.

The opening three trumpet notes of "Summertime" do me in—shadows of carefree love projected on a wall, sounds like creeping vines. They can strangle as well as bloom.

"Here," I say. "Here is a blooming flower."

It is not enough.

Too much.

I have started to call myself a Christian, and my friends don't understand why. I don't talk often of faith: the vexing fact of its existence, a splinter too small to see. In my circles, faith is something to be skeptical of, if not something to be frowned upon. I get it. I do. I agree. But still, my faith, like a weed, refuses to stay uprooted. It grows of its own accord. All it takes is disturbed soil and neglect. Then green shoots push their way up.

Kneeling on the sun-warmed wood because T once suggested that I might pray every day, I worry about policies ripping communities apart, about interminable wars, about climate change, injustice. If God won't fix that—if that's on us—what use is faith?

A tiny Christmas tree is already shedding its needles in the corner, and I am surrounded by fourteen people sitting on a hodgepodge of chairs, on cushions on the big rug on the floor, a lucky few perched on the faded blue couch. Paul, who is taking this seriously, is Israelite 1. Nora, who is taking this even more seriously, is Israelite 2. I am the narrator. We are performing the third and fourth lessons.

Me: "A cry went up from Israel."

Paul: "The people of Judah are in mourning."

Nora: "In her cities, we thirst for you. We lie on the cracked ground in sorrow."

Paul: "The doe abandons her fawn in the field. We stand on the hilltops and pant for breath like jackals, our eyes straining, seeking water, but there is none to be found."

Nora: "For as the deer pants after water, so pants my soul for God. You are the hope of Israel, the light of man, but to me, you are as a stranger."

Someone pokes Mooney, who is playing Isaiah.

Mooney: "Woe is me! I am undone. I am a man of unclean lips living among men of unclean lips. We feel the weight of man's injustice. We feel the bite of inequity, the hatred of our fellows, the weight of tyranny. We live without hope, without love, without you, O Lord."

Me: "God heard his people cry out to him, and his countenance shone upon them. He sent his seraphim to the prophet Isaiah—seraphim with six wings of silver and gold."

Gita is the angel. She nails her cue.

Gita: "Lo, I have touched your lips and purged your sin. Go and tell all God's people: Though they walk in darkness, they will see a great light. A light will dawn on those who dwell in the land of deep darkness, and they will rejoice at the harvest they will receive. The yoke of their burdens, the bar across their shoulders, the rod of their oppressors—all will break."

Me (laughing because Gita is making her voice high, bouncy, and angelic): "And Isaiah heard, and he obeyed, going forth and telling all."

Mooney: "For unto us a child is born; unto us a son is given. The government shall be upon his shoulders, and he shall be called Wonderful Counselor, the Mighty God, the Everlasting Father, the Prince of Peace. Of his greatness and justice there will be no end. He will reign upon David's throne and kingdom, and his righteousness will live on forever, lifting high the meek with one hand, and laying low the wicked with the other."

Gita: "The wolf shall dwell with the lamb; the leopard shall lie down with the kid; the calf and the young lion and the duckling shall be together; and a little child shall lead them. The cow and the bear shall feed; their young ones shall sleep side by side. The lion shall eat straw like the ox."

Paul (a little late): "Rejoice!"

Nora (right on time): "As the waters cover the sea, so shall the knowledge of the Lord be a blanket over all the earth."

After, Nora asks earnestly, "What do these lessons mean?" We pause and consider, but no one can answer satisfactorily.

We hold candles during "Silent Night," and Galen turns off the lights.

What use is faith? is a summer question.

Maybe redemption is not a place you find, but a system of mapmaking. Sketch a land. Pencil in dragons. Imagine it real, resplendent, and broken under a waxing moon.

CAROL

For L

I am mindlessly scrolling on my phone, and then I notice that I'm holding my breath. There I am, and there is L, from high school. Smiling and laughing, we are a mess of teenagers, arms wrapped around each other's shoulders. The picture lies. L is dead. I read the words her family uses—*depression* and *addiction* and *found peace*. These are my words.

The next day, I am surprised when I push open the office door on my midmorning break and the sunlight glares off the streaks on my glasses. I wipe them and call H. He picks up—second ring.

"John!" He sounds delighted. "How are you?"

I try to match his tone, but I practically shout his name in overcompensation. There is no preamble, and as I tell him about L's death, I realize how ridiculous I must sound.

"A girl I knew from high school, they found her body. She's dead, and I think she killed herself or overdosed." It comes out quickly. Hysterically. There is a long pause on the other end of the line.

"Surely you've known others," H says.

"Yeah," I say to him. "Yes—I don't know why this one hit me so hard."

"Were you close?" he asks.

"No," I say. "Not with her. I think I'm just tired."

"Well . . ." He trails off. He doesn't sound confused. He sounds like he's waiting for me to get to the point. "It's always hard."

"Why wasn't it me?" I say. I am asking about the extremities of weather.

He is silent a long while. "You going to meetings?" he asks.

I'm outside a just-closed coffee shop with V. We are talking about what it means to kill yourself. We are talking about loss. We are both already dead. This is only half a metaphor.

"I was thinking about L—just thinking about her—a couple of days before I found out," he says. "It keeps happening like this. I think about a person, then I find out they're dead. I'm gonna start calling folks just to make sure they're still alive."

I laugh, but the saliva in my mouth is metallic, and my heart is racing. I blurt out: "If push came to shove, I don't think I'd drink again, but I might kill myself."

"I know what you mean."

The distance between me and her seems not so far. She is there, and I am here, just across this river. But the High Bridge could not bring me to where I wanted to go. I could only stand in the middle of it. John Ashbery, inscribed on a bridge in Minneapolis: *It is so much like a beach after all, where you stand and think of going no further.* I could not cross without wanting to jump. I must have been just as foreign to her as she was to me.

Loss. The moment when I sum my memories of you and they do not make you.

AFTER CATULLUS

I am walking into a church basement when nausea inkblots out from my stomach. Everything is where it ought to be, but nothing is right. The posters on the wall haven't moved. The battered metal folding chairs still squeak on the lino-leum. The coffee remains black and burnt. Fickle familiarity can leave at any moment, it seems. Maybe we ought to keep a chair open for it, like a dead brother's seat at a communal table. And then I am at your tomb. (I am not literally at your tomb.) You are not here. (You are literally interred.) I bow my head and fold my hands and stay silent in your honor—a death-gift—because this is the only thing that ever bound you to me. (This is literally all I have.)

THE EIGHTH LESSON

They rejoiced.

Matthew 2:10

Galen and I sit on the couch, me holding the baby, Geryon nestled between us. We finish a Wednesday crossword puzzle together, the baby's eyes blinking, closing, shut tight. This actually happened.

I know that babies like high-contrast images, so I am eager to show her the moon cut out of the night sky—our moon, which we do not name (though it has a name) but call, simply, *the moon* just like I call her *the baby*.

"It's a perfect moon," Galen says.

"She's a perfect baby," the nurse says.

One night, looking up at the faint stars and hunting for a moon that refuses to be found, long after I've put the baby to bed, I grip the sharp plastic arms of our lawn chair because I am having a revelation that *not everything is precarious*. I ponder this for a while, and then I stand up because I am having another revelation that *everything is precarious, but that's OK*. I know I am exhausted because these thoughts are objectively banal, but I feel them as my stomach swoops and my head leavens. I can't fit the import of these concepts into words. Jack Gilbert: *How astonishing it is that language can almost mean, and frightening that it does not quite.*

The best night skies are like this—holding things so old, tired, and universal that we all can see ourselves in them, but drawn so skillfully that they shimmer with new, fresh, and singular understanding. One day soon, I will take this baby girl out to the porch, let her look up at the stars and moon and teach her the names of constellations, and tell her the stories of them, and she will not understand because she is preverbal and can see only eight to twelve inches in front of her face.

The baby writhes in my arms as we call her name after name.
She cries at them all, and, for once, I don't mind it.

From New York, I move back to Minneapolis, where I live with my sister, Sarah, in what should be her daughter's room, but her daughter is young enough to sleep with her, so I lie diagonally on a too-small bed with floral sheets, and Dora the Explorer judges me from the wall. This begins the happiest period of my adult life.

Sarah and I are like a sitcom on a shoestring budget. The set is always the porch. Her five-month-old coos and scuttles around while we learn about siblinghood. There are no loose ends: all the conflicts wrap themselves up before the closing credits.

I sit outside Sarah's house, coding, with my back to the wall, like a cat in the sunlight. I become friends with the mailman. I am not lonely, even though I know few people in my hometown, even though my few remaining friends from high school have drifted away, even though my friends from college are putting down their wiry roots elsewhere, in the great metropolises of America.

I remeet V, who is cynical now that we are no longer high schoolers. V was something of a terror then—a boy in a long line of boys to be avoided. He is still loud and quick with judgments, but quicker with salty smiles. When he says something he doesn't like, he pretends to vomit into his hand. We swig coffee at shops I barely remember all around this city that was once mine. I go to his birthday party at the house he owns—people my age own houses in this city!—and he fires up the grill in his backyard and talks and laughs with all kinds. Everyone is sober. I meet T, who is as solid as an oak beam. He will come to call me brother, and I will find I like that.

I buy a used bike. Refurbished and baby blue, it's all I need. Louise Erdrich, the famous author, owns a bookstore that is blocks away, so I ride over and buy too many of her books. Sometimes I stop at the upscale restaurant next door to get iced coffee. My bike doesn't have a cup holder, so I pedal one-handed, swerving around the nearly empty streets of my neighborhood at odd hours. Sarah buys me a book about biking.

I bike to meetings. I bike to lake after lake and dip my toes in each one. I bike down the bike highway, just to see how far I can go, for the sheer joy of it, and the pedals stop working. I don't crash but come to a slow, pathetic stop. The whole pedal mechanism seems to have fallen away from the frame. It hangs limp and useless. I know something is wrong with the bottom bracket—a word I just learned. I have no idea what it might be. I say *fuck* too loudly for this respectable lakeside neighborhood, and I call my brother because Sarah is out of town. While I wait for him to come and get me, I smoke on a bench and stare at my bicycle, which lies on a heap in the cool grass. I stare it down with all the intensity I can muster, as though I might shame it back to life. It stays twisted and broken on the ground.

My brother arrives, throws my bike into the back of his minivan, and we talk about bad sci-fi shows while he drives me home. The next day, I go to the bike store; they fix my bike; and I pedal around, happy once again. This happened, but it is also a metaphor.

On a bench by a lake in the heart of Minneapolis, the whole city out walking, I read Louise Erdrich: *Let yourself sit by an apple tree and listen to the apples falling all around you in heaps, wasting their sweetness. Tell yourself you tasted as many as you could.*

I'm listening. Maybe I am Tantalus in a hell of my own devising. But maybe I'm not. Maybe I'll reach for this fruit, now close enough to grasp, now cool in my hand, now hard against my teeth, finally crisp, then sweet, on my tongue.

Every Tuesday, I bike down to the coffee shop on Hennepin Avenue where T and I discuss what it means to be redeemed. I read aloud from the Big Book, and he stops me to ask if I have any questions. I don't often, but when I do, he nods seriously, silent before he answers. I can see him hauling up the wisdom at the end of the chain of men who came before him. An anchor breaking the dark surface, green with age.

I go to a hospital and talk to teens about sobriety. After, I want to drink only the feeling of being useful.

Then I'm on the Lake Street bus, and I see a man who could be Y. Suddenly, I am with Y again, back in the basement of our halfway house, playing pool. Solids stack up in pockets, and he doesn't tire of beating me, of correcting my play. We talk about his troubles, and I realize that redemption is being built around me so slowly, I can almost think I'm doing the work myself. Its bricks are quarried from the harm I did, cut, precisely, into perceived wisdom. Y couldn't put his black-market jobs on his résumé, couldn't afford to go to a sober house after this. I get to be One of the Good Ones; he gets to be who people like me are compared to. The injustice of redemption, its hollowness, slaps me again.

But in my mind, I give everyone on that bus another chance. "You get another chance," I say. "You get another chance too." I want to be like Oprah: "You and you and you." When I get off, I thank the driver and give her another chance also. Can we make redemption big enough for everyone—or do we need something new?

The words *sin* and *trespasses* are loaded, and the King James has it as *debts* anyway, so *debts* is what I've learned to say. Those debts that I incur are of the sort that can't be paid back. Since redemption is not a given moment but an ongoing practice, I take my medication every day and brush my teeth before I go to bed. I try not to take out new loans.

Madeleine L'Engle: *All will be redeemed in God's fullness of time. All, not just the small portion of the population who have been given the grace to know and accept Christ. All the strayed and stolen sheep. All the little lost ones.*

I may yet be redeemed, but I am too impatient to wait for death.

I start attending Quaker services—an attempt to quiet myself in case God is talking. I haven't heard anything yet. The talk of Jesus leaves me cold, but a warm glow moves outward from my chest when a man asks, *Are we motivated by fear or by love?* The question isn't rhetorical, but in a Quaker meeting, when someone is moved to speak, you aren't supposed to answer their question directly. Still, I say silently, *More and more by love.*

Just because you don't respond directly doesn't mean there is no conversation, no through line. Sometimes two messages never touch but still connect.

I visit Chicago, where Alice lives with Galen, a mutual friend from college. I edited, once, a long piece of Galen's about queerness and walking and food. We fought over every adjective, and I remember it fondly.

What does it mean to regret something? This is the question that animates us. It is not idle. Every seven years, David notes, every cell that was once us has been replaced. This frightens me, but I am exhilarated all the same.

Galen and I talk late into the night in the backyard of their three-flat apartment building. We are sitting on this bench, touching the narrow points of each other's regret, when a rocket goes up as in the opening lick of a Bach cantata. The fireworks sound joyous, but we can't see them. I remember a hotel room on a drive between Ohio and Minnesota, where I sat on the bed and read the first poem I'd ever read of Galen's. It was about cicadas, though it was really about death. Later, I met her in person, with some mutual friends, at a greasy pizza place near our rural college. We went bowling, watched *The Breakfast Club*. Galen tells me that the poem I read in that hotel room was not, in fact, really about death.

How many notes in a Bach cantata need to change before it's a different piece altogether? What lives in the center of a piece? I tell Galen that Bach used to write many versions of the same piece, and now a cottage industry of musicologists turns out singular versions, *real* and *authentic*, from the plastic of composition. Daniel Melamed: *Someone, whether an editor or a performer, has to choose, because as a rule one cannot perform multiple versions of a work. . . . Ultimately, this comes down to opinion or esthetic judgement, not objective truth.* So we are already talking about form, about the limits and joys of it, about the difference between what we put on the world (composition numbers, grammar) and what is already there (music, concepts). But I am not really talking about a Bach cantata or language—at least not these things only. I'm really talking about me.

The report of a firecracker. "I hate fireworks," Galen says. We go inside.

We all go dancing at an event loosely related to librarians at a bar in a hip Chicago neighborhood. Not one of us is a librarian. David teaches a librarian with short red hair and green overalls how to move her hands the way he does. He winds them in and out slowly, precisely. "See?" he asks. She smiles and laughs, and I recognize, with an ache, the unmistakable signs of flirtation. Galen and I, giggling, get our pictures taken at the photo booth. We smile at the camera, and my hand is over her belly, and her hand is over my hand. Feeling mischievous, I post the pictures online. But when I get confused messages asking who this person is and if we're expecting, I feel like an idiot.

Galen and I write every day. I develop a Pavlovian response to the chime my computer makes when she types *hi*. This is computer-mediated romance, but it is not awful. It is not like OkCupid. She tells me that she's charting her first kiss with everyone she's ever kissed. I am on this kiss list, from college: a Scorpio, three years older than her, rated a three out of four (for kiss enjoyment). It's disappointing that she confirms my experience: our kiss was fine. Our two and a half dates were fine.

The friendship that resulted is good, though, so we decide to make an interactive website. I build charts and graphs of her romances: *How intoxicated was she? How much shame did she feel? How much did she regret it?* We graduate to phone calls, and I walk down to Lake of the Isles, picnic alone, stroll down paths where the goose shit coats my shoes. In the thick, warm night, I sit beneath a crabapple tree on top of the hill I used to sled down as a child. The dense fruit will fall soon.

Then, suddenly, Galen and I are on a dock in rural Wisconsin. Her roommates are up in the cabin, and the light spills out from its porch, gets caught on the trees, makes complicated patterns on the surface of the still, black water. The moon is only a sliver, but the stars are out in force, the long arm of the Milky Way just visible.

"There is a moment," Galen says, "when you leave Earth's atmosphere, and then you're in space, and you can't come back."

"Can I kiss you?" I ask.

"Yes," she says.

I move to Chicago. On my birthday, Galen makes apple crumble from the remains of autumn's harvest, the last of the season's sweetness.

"*Tell yourself you tasted as many as you could,*" she says.

I stay with Galen while we look for an apartment for me. "I don't like this one," she says to a garden-level one-bedroom with granite countertops and a dishwasher. "No light." Eventually, I find a place in a small apartment building. On the fourth floor, it commands a view of the neighborhood and the highway. Its walls are painted yellow. Its wood molding is stained dark. Its rooms are placed strangely. One investigative Sunday afternoon, holding a tape measure triumphantly, Galen discovers that it is 510 square feet excluding the bathroom.

Sarah gave me an air mattress. It has a slow leak, but Galen and I lie on it together and watch *Better Off Dead* on my computer. We take turns reinflating it in the middle of the night. I grow accustomed to groggily moving my car from one side of the street to another every time we sleep in her apartment. We call this Endless Sleepover. We have sex multiple times a day. Whenever it is especially good, we celebrate by going to a New York–style pizza place that plays, exclusively, death metal.

Then, a condom breaks. We are calm, collected, as we talk about what we're going to do. We walk briskly to the pharmacy. The line is long. We wait with frozen impatience. Finally, Galen holds eye contact with the pharmacy technician, who is in her twenties like us. Then we are back at her apartment, and Galen is crying so much, and nothing I can say is helpful, and she will cry forever, and it's no one's fault, but it's also my fault. She sobs silently, like a muted television. I hold her.

Chicago charms me. In the gold autumn glow of this new city, the baristas in the coffee shop make me feel old and wise even though I am still in my twenties. I fail to memorize my new neighbors' names again and again. I watch a stooped man use a broom to shoo a chicken off the awning above his door.

I learn Galen's neighborhood too. The person who serves me coffee at the too-small bakery with the too-large parking lot where I can turn my car around. The employees of the corner deli who sell me discounted cigarettes. The game Galen's roommates play with the magnets on their fridge.

On lazy weekend mornings, Galen and I spend hours in bed debating how quickly to move in together. We're both on the same side of the fight. *Let's take this slowly*, we say. Then our books appear on each other's shelves, mixed together chemically, inseparable.

I am sober, but I never intended to be sober. I am happy, but I always thought happiness would be mundane.

It is summer again, and Galen and I are driving back up to Wisconsin, where my family has gathered. We have been together for almost exactly one year. Galen is late, but not so very late. A week maybe. I never liked dares, but, by silent agreement, we dare each other the whole drive up— we imagine names for our unborn child, picture its little feet kicking.

We stop at a CVS and now she is peeing on a stick, and I am waiting outside scared both that she is and isn't.

I am scared that we are and aren't.

She isn't.
 We aren't.
  Do we want to be?

Galen and I walk down to the square with its eagle-headed obelisk. We go to a store that sells Chicago-made clothes and trinkets. We buy two brass rings. We each put one on.

My boss calls to see if I can do a late meeting. I tell her I just got engaged.

"Oh my god!" she exclaims.

I don't go to the meeting.

We eat an early dinner at a place with wood-fired pizza and sit at an outdoor table on the sidewalk. Two of our friends walk by, and we talk breathless and excited. Galen doesn't want to tell people yet. Not our friends, certainly. Not even her family. But I don't hide the ring—such a little rose-gold thing, they won't see it. I take a long drink from my ginger ale. The glass bottle presses the metal deep into my finger, and I have to work to steady my voice.

When we call Galen's parents, they are silent for several seconds. Their caution smothers our excitement. They ask us to wait to tell the rest of the family. Galen goes to a yard sale seemingly out of a Borges story where the prices for items are measured in degrees of anger. She buys hot pink skin-tight shorts for three screams. It's cathartic, I think, to let anger out.

Everyone is confounded. She has been with women. I have been with men. We are young, and we haven't been dating that long. Our friends aren't getting married. Maybe they'll never get married because the institution is rotten and patriarchal and monogamy is a farce. *Yes*, we say. *Yes, that's true*, but we'll make it ours anyway. My friends might disapprove, but they let me convince them of my determination.

Like, "what if you get divorced?" David asks.

"Then we get divorced," I say.

"Then what's the point of getting married at all—I mean, if you can just get unmarried?"

The point of getting married, I decide, is to tie ourselves to the long line of people in union who came before us, to have a moment where we visibly hold hands and step into the future together, where our family and friends can see us. This wedding is for them—to whom I never showed this side of myself, this part that craved companionship. It is for Galen. Yes, it is for me too.

The church is not air-conditioned. I wear mostly white linen, which is supposed to breathe, but there are three layers, and the vest does not breathe because it is not linen, so sweat is matting my hair and dripping into my eyes, and I have to remember not to lock my knees or I will faint.

In the foyer, I hear the music I wrote, the music that set some of LC's wedding poems for organ, recorder, and voice. "I am never doing this again," Molly sings. She sings *again* over and over (this kind of literalism is a trope in text setting); the word rings over and over like wedding bells. Maybe I will do this again. We are married, but we might one day be unmarried. But I will never do *this* again, I decide.

When we walk in, Molly sings an aria from a Bach cantata that I love. Clea and a woman I don't know play the recorder. Jacob plays the organ. It is lovely; I have never heard music more lovely. I notice it, and I do not notice it. I have crossed into some state beyond calm and focused where I have never been before.

Our siblings read poems as I look out at my friends and family and the waving sea of hand-fans. Sarah starts, reading Robert Hass. Dan reads E. E. Cummings. John reads Marge Piercy. Andrew, Jack Gilbert.

Then Kath is reading Galen, tearing up. Galen Beebe: *Grain on grain on grain on grain on grain.* I do not tear up, which surprises me. I am always tearing up at everything. Galen is used to it by now. When I sniffle, watching some trite television show, she pats whatever part of me she can reach, but she keeps her face glued to the television. But now, I am not crying.

Later, we rush out of the church doors to the Widor Toccata. The quick arpeggios, the rough jabs of chords in the pedals, the sense of building wonderment: the song lifts me up, bodily hurls me from the church in one long run of joy. My mouth will not close; it is spread open in a surprised smile that won't leave.

Our friends cry. After we sign the paperwork, Karim grabs my head and puts our foreheads against each other. Galen and I have just vowed to try to love ourselves as much as we love each other. I find that I want to struggle this way. It puts the burden in the right place.

LC and I are half in the too-hot hot tub, talking about things we are afraid of, and I mention a particular kind of cancer that turns you into an asshole—takes away your filter, changes your personality. LC thinks this makes sense. I ask them why.

"Because," they say, "you think you're a monster, and your greatest fear is that everyone will figure it out."

A didn't want to be *A with speed*. She didn't want to be *A with AA* either. She just wanted *to be*, and I envy her certainty that there is some way *to be*, absent our rusted pasts. So what lives at the center of a piece of music? Or in the heart of a poem? Or the soul of a person? No, tigers never change their stripes. No, old dogs can't learn new tricks. These are good as far as idioms go, but let's see what happens to monsters.

I laughed, of course, when I heard on some podcast that a dove is actually the same kind of bird as a pigeon. But we don't release pigeons at weddings, the host noted dryly. The line between these two imagined species is a question of aesthetics and nomenclature—a question of beauty—not a question of truth.

Galen and I collect houseguests around Christmas, and it's only sometimes on purpose. Raffi calls. He's on his way back to Vermont. He was in North Dakota—in Standing Rock—working in the kitchens of the camp there. Can he stay with us for a couple of days?

Since the Manhattan diner with LC only a few days ago, I've had Christmas tunes stuck in my head. I used up all my goodwill with Galen to listen to the Roches' Christmas album, a family tradition, on loop. It was worth Galen's long-suffering sigh. Since then, I've been humming hymns, singing tunes, whistling melodies, hammering out carols on the keyboard, strumming the chords to "The Coventry Carol" on my battered ukulele (a gift from Alice the year before).

"There are only two radio stations in North Dakota," Raffi reports. "They were both playing goddamn Christmas tunes the whole drive here."

Raffi doesn't look at me too hard, but I know what he's saying: *Maybe stop humming "Have Yourself a Merry Little Christmas."* I stop.

"I know I'm a grinch," Raffi says. He's not a grinch. I wonder sometimes at his heart, two sizes too big. "But Christmas is just *consumerism.*"

Tall, with a rough fabric shirt and a literal rope for a belt, Raffi sees Christmas as little more than a capitalist mystery play. I get it, but I'm still defensive. I search for the right words and settle on the Bible.

"And the Word was made flesh and dwelt among us," I say.

"There are moments," Galen, a reluctant congregant, quotes me quoting Robert Hass, "when the body is as numinous as words."

"Christmas," I lecture, "is that moment—the moment when we realize that our words, hopes, ideas, need to and do take on a physical dimension." Raffi's silence is polite. I feel like a zealot. "It means that we need to take action, make material change to make the world just."

"That's nice," Raffi says. He says it with feeling. The conversation moves on. An hour later, I catch myself humming "Have Yourself a Merry Little Christmas" again.

"The Coventry Carol" is a dirge about Herod killing a bunch of kids. Real Christmas is sad Christmas.

The words to "Have Yourself a Merry Little Christmas" confuse everyone. The song first appeared with Judy Garland performing it in *Meet Me in St. Louis* (1944), and when Garland sang it, it was *until then we'll have to muddle through somehow*. In Frank Sinatra's cover (arguably more famous than the original), it was *hang a shining star up on the highest bough*. Finding out which way you ought to sing the last stanza involves understanding the context in which the different versions were written—as well as the context in which you want to perform it now. That is, there's no answer to the question *which is the* real *last stanza?* There's only figuring out why one might be a better fit. And, anyway, even if there is a *real* last stanza, it wouldn't necessarily equal a *better* one.

Hugh Martin, the song's writer, seems to have given interviews to half the planet about "Have Yourself a Merry Little Christmas," and I discover that the earlier Garland version is not, in fact, the first version of the song. In the Garland version, the line *until then we'll have to muddle through somehow* is brought in with *Someday soon we all will be together / if the Fates allow*. In the original, which Garland (and the director of *Meet Me in St. Louis*) found far too dark, that line is framed with *But at last we all will be together / if the Lord allows*. In the rewrite, we have a charming line about making it until their loved ones are back. In the original, we get a Sunday school lesson about how we'll all meet again when we're dead. *Meet Me in St. Louis* came out during World War II. As the critic Bruce Handy writes in the *New York Times*: *Amid loss, separation and uncertainty, lyrics from Martin's softened rewrite . . . were poignant enough.*

Almost every line of Martin's song changed after Garland refused to sing it. The first stanza was so bleak that it was almost funny: *Have yourself a merry little Christmas. / It may be your last.* Now it's *Let your heart be light*, which is still sad, I suppose. For the words to implore it, your heart must not be light to begin with.

When does a song change so much that it becomes a different song altogether? This is not an idle question; I'm really asking, *have I changed so much that I have become a different person altogether?* Is the me that once was dead? Am I born anew? In high school, my English teacher put us on the hunt for resurrection stories—the *real* story of a book, it seemed, was always full of Christ imagery. Death and rebirth.

Garland thought the song was too sad. So did Sinatra. I think it was too sad too, but that's not the real problem. It was on the nose. Without depth. Unwilling to own up to what it means to be sad.

Showing off for Raffi, Galen and I invite over some friends, do our best impressions of foodies. Everything is local, from the CSA and farmer's market. We milled the wheat for the bread in our electric wheat mill.

H laughs. "You're parodies of yourselves."

"They pet these chickens before they kill them," I say without guile.

He laughs harder.

The nice thing about having my life mistaken for a parody is that there's something real there to parody at all.

Being in Chicago, after all, is an accident. An accident that Galen heard from the job there before she heard from the one in San Francisco. An accident that Alice, then, moved in with Galen in Chicago. An accident that I, then, visited Alice on a lark and fell in love with Galen. But from all the contingency emerges something solid. Useful to have this realization before we leave Chicago, before we move once again.

I get sick the night before the Nine Lessons and Carols—a ball of snot and stress, and I am so tired. We have it at Alice's house because we've finally outgrown our own apartment. Twenty-one people come, which is more than we've ever had, and we sing and hold candles, and I choke up a little while playing the keyboard. Everyone holds their books, and a friend plays electric bass, and the singing is off key, but no one cares. Soon we will get on a plane and leave Chicago. I am happy—though I know that isn't the right word—in this sad season of Christmastime. Happier than I ever have been.

At an Easter Quaker meeting, months later, a woman will note that the world was fallen when Jesus died on the cross, and that the world is fallen still. Some debts can't be paid back. But tonight, as Galen and I slide into a taxi, return to our mess of an apartment, overflowing with things to be given away or taken to the dump, my eyes shine like Judy Garland's, and a wild and strange hope leaks out. I may still be redeemed in God's fullness of time, but on this earth—fortunately for one as impatient as me—there will always be cause for Christmas.

CAROL

For A

I am driving across state lines, listening to music, when a sadness gnaws its way out of my chest and crawls into the passenger seat next to me. On my right, I feel the release of A's absence, the ongoing sensation of weight just lifted from my side.

I am remembering her mussed hair, plastered at odd angles. I am remembering her sudden grace in the modern dance class. I am remembering the porch on the sober house in Saint Paul with chipped white paint and green plastic furniture and the Mississippi just blocks away. I am remembering laughing, running across the thin strip of road that separates us from the dense forest just before the river, pushing our way through the underbrush that snares our clothes, down the hill, deeper into the forest, and then the water. And then she's gone.

But I am bored of grief, even as it sits and stares with its bright, animal eyes.

Then, I am sitting with friends who never knew me when I drank. The wind brings up little waves that alternate bright blue and soft gold in the late afternoon light. LC is explaining with words I do not have to the others: "What you need to understand is that a lot of people just fade away."

"They die?" another friend asks.

"Maybe," LC answers. "They just kind of go away. Dead, maybe. Into the gutter, maybe. Just *away*. They disappear from your life."

In this moment, I realize I am making a memory. Making a memory of a memory of A. Each iteration of her, laid out in a line, less corporeal than the last. Loss lurks between each, stretching back to the first—a real person with a body and agency. A recitation of a poem of a feeling. A screenshot of a screenshot. An essay.

Each one of her has a hold on me.

In rural Vermont, I sit on the farmhouse porch and watch my friends swim across the slow-moving water that divides us from New Hampshire. I see their naked bodies scramble up the bank, into the dark pines, then disappear.

Galen wants to write about this place, about the liminal spaces between us and the dead. She reads from her essay in the barn, the sun pouring in through the irregular gaps in the warped, centuries-old boards. *These are my words*, she declares. There are dancers in the barn because we are at an artists' colony. One walks slowly across the room in time to the music that directs her movements. She walks across the room and pounds her chest. These are my words, because my gift is not for the dead.

Grief is lossy. In the absence of a body to touch or a voice to speak with, how could it not be? Still, I will give you all the poems I have to offer, because here is one word, and here is another, and they are more carefully arranged than I can bear.

A is sitting on the porch of her sober house, reading me a poem about birds, which, she later will tell me, is really a poem about an ex, which, I know now, is really a poem about loss. *Loss.* The time we sat on the porch and I listened to a poem about birds.

On Christmas, every year, I'll read Hass's words aloud to the friends who have traveled through snow to come to our home. *There are moments when the body is as numinous / as words, days that are the good flesh continuing.* Jesus's body is as numinous as words, I'll say. Even though the story remains improbable, I'll find it beautiful every year. I'll believe it more and more. We'll light candles, and Galen will turn off the lights. We'll raise the candles above our heads. Into the silence, I'll read the passage from John—*And the Word was made flesh and dwelt among us*—and together we will hope the words we have into bodies, and pray they make a person as whole as we recall. *Such tenderness, those afternoons and evenings, / saying* blackberry, blackberry, blackberry.

AFTER CATULLUS

At the communal table, we leave a chair open. A man sneaks in late, but the door slams behind him, and red takes his face and ears. He sees the open chair in this church basement, but we will not let him sit in it. "Over there," someone whispers. I have been this man, an occupational hazard of a career of excess. Then we grasp hands and speak words I know by heart. How senseless, the violence of fate which has cleaved us, and all it left me was prayer.

THE NINTH LESSON

And the Word was made flesh and dwelt among us.

John 1:14

The sun is down. And then, suddenly, it's not. Yellow cracks spread all across the surface of the water—a dark mass only minutes before. Tonight the cat will kill a mouse, leave it for us to find tomorrow. Now she is rubbing her neck against the door from the porch back into the kitchen. This is her house. The book is heavy in my hands this early. The rocking chair leaned all the way back, my feet up on a coffee table—I am on the very edge of Vermont. I could swim to New Hampshire. This afternoon, everyone but me will. I will sit and watch the naked figures of my friends scramble up the brown bank and disappear into the pines.

At this place, the mornings are wordless, at least until the meditation is over. I can hear the sounds of the others moving from their bedrooms to the bathroom to the kitchen. The harsh flush of the toilet, the gentle gurgle of the coffee carafe. Everything is fused with a sense of unreality. Being unable to name my emotional state to the others makes my feelings seem not just unknown but unknowable.

Everyone else is sitting cross-legged or on their knees under the thin shade of the pear tree, but my back is stiff, shooting pain down my right arm, so I lie down, the shadows passing over my closed eyes. I know the tall grass is moving. I can feel the touch of the breeze. The sun warms my face.

Galen nudges me with me her bare foot, and my eyes burst open, and everyone is smiling with their eyes closed. I have been snoring. I don't know about this meditation practice, about this temporary abandonment of naming, but I close my eyes and think about communion, about the petrified rodent body they discovered in the basement of the shit-heaped barn, untouched for years. I think about the wagon they found. About the long boards of wood from trees hundreds of years old when they were cut. I think about the wrong names in Jack Gilbert's poem, the astonishing way they almost mean, the trembling fear that comes because they do not quite.

Later, I peel off Galen's thin cotton shirt, white like gesso. The afternoon light passes through the shirt caught on her arms above her head, turning it gold and malleable. We try, unsuccessfully, to muffle laughter, but we don't really speak. After, we fall asleep, our skin sticking together. Gilbert says that love is honey, giraffes are desire in the dark. I want to know where under the dark choppy surface of language his poem finds purchase. I won't ever know. I must learn to have faith that it does.

But depression is a moon in a perfect orbit, always moving, never closer to or further from its object, which is my own broken self. Today I wake to the baby's cry, and I resent the hoarseness in her voice. I resent that I didn't wake at the first sound, that I slept till she wailed. I resent the reminder that I am not the man I want to be.

After I feed her, we go to the porch, and I lay her down on a stack of towels and drink my coffee while she coos at the sun that passes through the leaves of the neighbor's oak. The questions I have can't be answered by rustling trees or chattering squirrels. I ask them anyway. That's prayer for you, I guess.

These days, I crave a garden. But why? I want something to tend, but it's improbable that I would, in fact, tend a garden, since I only barely tend myself. But still, I can see myself picking a slug off a leaf, weeding around the herbs, watering the whole face of my little ground. The truth is that I want a garden in the same way I want God: because of the beauty contained in its improbability.

I look out at my neighbor's garden, verdant, and a future sadness fills me. When my depression comes back, I will fail my garden, cease to tend the things that give me joy. But then the baby cries and needs a bottle, and besides, I know, *accept things I cannot change*, etc.

It used to be that in a tragedy, you died, and in a comedy, you got hitched, so I feel the urge to exit this story with the wedding. But this fact remains: I still sometimes want to die.

Prayer is an awful narrative device because it ends either in deus ex machina or futility. But, still, I pray that my lost friends will get sober, that I will stay sober, that this baby will live her life unconcerned with sobriety. While I pray, I know a thousand other men, just like me, are on their knees praying, mostly for stupid things, or selfish things, things that probably won't come to pass, but the thought heartens me anyway.

I pick the baby up, feed her a bottle, and burp her. Billions of people have burped their babies. Billions of people have prayed. Joy in life, if there is any joy in life, comes when one does away with the idea that originality is a virtue—or even possible. Someday, maybe, I'll surrender to that and take my place as an orderer of psalms and not a psalmist.

The baby closes her eyes, and I kneel to pray once more. God doesn't respond, but the words of my prayer interlock with the words of all the others, and maybe everyone prays for stupid, impossible things—I don't know.

"You use a lot of quotations," a friend says. "Why are you hiding behind their words?"

That question makes sense only if the point of art is out there in plain sight. This is to say, prayer is useless, but only if the point of prayer is up in heaven. But I don't really know the point of prayer, and the baby is crying, and I don't know what to do myself, with my resentful, irredeemable self. So I read Psalm 5: *You cover the righteous with favor as with a shield.* But there is no shield against the tears, and why should there be? There's nothing to cover—just me and a baby and God together in this apartment while the sun stretches its legs before climbing up the sky.

Someone tells me that writing is always in service of either getting laid or getting even. Maybe, I think—but only if it's possible to get even with yourself.

Sitting on my porch after the whole neighborhood has gone to bed, unable to find my headphones, I let my phone's speaker bleat out a Bach cantata. "*Seufzer, Tränen, Kummer, Not, / Ängstlichs Sehnen, Furcht und Tod / Nagen mein beklemmtes Herz,*" a soprano sings. She and the oboe take turns leaping off a minor cliff, down and down. They each feint at resolutions, only to continue the unwinding melody. I make the mistake of looking up the translation: *Sighs, tears, grief, distress, longing, fear, and death prey upon my oppressed heart.* Oh, Bach.

It's late, and Bach is maudlin. I am maudlin, and I'm not sure who I am without my sadness. Without my disease. Without my resentment. Sometimes, I pray that I'll want to pray. Sometimes I believe that I believe in God. Sometimes I imagine a healthier imagination. John Calvin: *God is invisible—not only to the eyes, but also to the understandings of men. He is revealed to us in Christ alone, that we may behold him as in a mirror.* If God is invisible, what use is he? If Christ is our mirror, what use are we? *What use is faith?* might be a summer question, but what am I to do in this flowering season of my discontent?

The baby goes to daycare. I go to work. The baby learns *da da*. I swoon. The baby cries. I take ketamine. Time grinds on, sometimes quickly, sometimes slowly, change always materializing, despite itself. Despite me. Because of me. Both.

It is almost spring. The day has—and I can finally notice it!—stopped retreating from the night, but I want Christmas to come again already. A blizzard just passed through last night. This morning, I can barely recognize the cars and fire hydrants and trees and eaves of roofs beneath their freshly laundered blankets of snow. The baby clambers up the stool by the window and looks out with reverence, and then with excitement, pointing and shouting. I shovel the walk as she wades through banks as high as her chest, laughing. I give her a toy shovel which she scrapes along the ground with the same determination she brings to each new skill. People tell me things—absurd things, things about seeing with baby's eyes, etc.—and, today, I don't resent that I am, sometimes, seeing what she sees.

But that doesn't mean I don't desire Christmas.

The night of our Lessons and Carols, Galen and I pass the baby from lap to lap while, on the computer, a grid of family and friends sing along to "Have Yourself a Merry Little Christmas," their mute lips moving out of time but somehow in unison all the same. I am moved—as I am always moved by Christmas—and the presence of the baby changes everything and nothing, just as everything always changes, even as it remains stubbornly the same. It doesn't escape me that I enact the same ritual every year about how everything is going to be different. We promise, every time, that *the wolf shall dwell with the lamb*—but when? We say that *the lion shall eat straw like the ox*—but how?

Maybe I want Christmas not because its promises are empty but because they are waiting for us to fill them.

And time—stubborn as always—grinds on.

The baby, suddenly a toddler, runs across the backyard, over to the raised bed I built, shaded in the afternoon by the neighbor's oak. She pokes her nose into leaves of the mint plant and inhales.

"Mmm," she says.

"Mmm," I agree, replicating her sniff.

The swallows in the oak make some particularly loud chirps, and the toddler points up at its branches.

"Bird," she exclaims, delighted.

"I see," I say. "I see."

ACKNOWLEDGMENTS

Galen Beebe is my partner in nearly everything—and my first and best editor. Thank you, Galen, for all of it. Lauren Clark told me that a book is just a piece of wood touched so often that it has become smooth. Thank you, LC, for that wisdom, and for being a hand that touched this block of wood. I've lost count of the number of times David Ohana has read this book, as well as the number of times he's come through with some necessary bit of feedback. Thank you, David, for your patience and faith.

Thank you, Susan Cheever, Sven Birkerts, Peter Trachtenberg, Jenny Boully, and the faculty, staff, and students of the Bennington Writing Seminars, who cajoled, prompted, challenged, and encouraged this book. Thank you, Amber Bacon, Molly Bradley, Amelia Brown, Frances Greathead, Chelsea Hodson, Caitlin McGill, Kevin O'Meara, Britt Peterson, William Powers, Kate Rowe, Nora Sharp, Jennifer Solheim, Zachary Spence, and the many other writers, friends, and strangers who read and gave feedback while this book was in various stages of construction. Thank you, Lisa Ann Cockrel, Laurel Draper, and the entire team at Eerdmans, and Cassie Mannes Murray, who saw what I was trying to do and incarnated these words into paper and ink.

Thank you, my friends, my siblings, and my parents. I am ceaselessly grateful for all your love and support.

Thank you to the people—named and unnamed—in this book.

Thank God for fellowship and community.

And thank you, Lavinia, for *then, suddenly* making me a dad.

SOME NOTES ON THE TEXT

Many names have been changed to protect the privacy of the people in this book.

All of the quotations from the Bible were drawn originally from the King James Version. In all, I modernized the language. In many, I adapted them in order to highlight what drew me to the passage. This is particularly true of the epigraphs to each lesson.

On page 44, I adapted existing translations of Bach's *Actus tragicus* (BWV 106). The cited lines draw from biblical passages and Martin Luther. The translation of Bach's "Seufzer, Tränen, Kummer, Not" from BWV 21 is similarly adapted. Its original German text is by Salomon Franck.

"Self-Portrait in a Convex Mirror," copyright © 1974 by John Ashbery. Originally appeared in "Poetry"; from *Self-Portrait in a Convex Mirror* by John Ashbery. Used by permission of Viking Books, an imprint of Penguin Publishing Group, a division of Penguin Random House LLC. All rights reserved.

"Ars Poetica," from *Grace Notes* by Rita Dove. Copyright © 1989 by Rita Dove. Used by permission of W. W. Norton & Company, Inc.

"Meditation at Lagunitas," from *Praise* by Robert Hass. Copyright © 1979 by Robert Hass. Used by permission of HarperCollins Publishers.

SUGGESTED CAROLS

First lesson: "Once in Royal David's City" by Cecil Frances Alexander, 19th century.

Second lesson: "The Coventry Carol," anonymous, 16th century.

Third and fourth lessons: "Lo, How a Rose E'er Blooming," anonymous, 16th century; Theodore Baker, translator, 19th century.

Fifth lesson: "Gabriel's Message Does Away," anonymous, ca. 13th century; John Mason Neale, translator, 19th century.

Sixth lesson: "The Cherry Tree Carol," anonymous, 16th century.

Seventh lesson: "I Wonder as I Wander," collected by John Jacob Niles from Annie Morgan, 20th century.

Eighth lesson: "We Three Kings" by John Henry Hopkins Jr., 19th century.

Ninth lesson: "Silent Night" by Joseph Mohr, 19th century; John Freeman Young, translator, 19th century.